VALUES in CONFLICT

Christian
Nursing
in a
Changing
Profession

▶

Judith Allen Shelly
& Arlene B. Miller

INTERVARSITY PRESS
DOWNERS GROVE, ILLINOIS 60515

InterVarsity Press is the book-publishing division of InterVarsity Christian Fellowship, a student movement active on campus at hundreds of universities, colleges and schools of nursing in the United States of America, and a member movement of the International Fellowship of Evangelical Students. For information about local and regional activities, write Public Relations Dept., InterVarsity Christian Fellowship, 6400 Schroeder Rd., P.O. Box 7895, Madison, WI 53707-7895.

All Scripture quotations, unless otherwise indicated, are from the Holy Bible, New International Version. Copyright © 1973, 1978, International Bible Society. Used by permission of Zondervan Bible Publishers.

Scripture quotations denoted by NRSV are from the New Revised Standard Version Bible, copyright 1989 by the Division of Christian Education of the National Council of the Churches of Christ in the USA and used by permission.

Cover illustration: Roberta Polfus

ISBN 0-8308-1330-6

Printed in the United States of America

Library of Congress Cataloging-in-Publication Data

Shelly, Judith Allen.
    Values in conflict: Christian nursing in a changing profession/
Judith Allen Shelly & Arlene B. Miller.
        p.   cm.
    Includes bibliographical references.
    ISBN 0-8308-1330-6
    1. Nursing—Religious aspects—Christianity.   2. Nursing
ethics.
    I. Miller, Arlene B., 1935-   . II. Title. III. Title: Christian
nursing in a changing profession.
    [DNLM: 1. Christianity.   2. Ethics, Nursing.   WY 85 S545v]
    85.2.S54   1991
    248.8'8—dc20
    DLC
    for Library of Congress   91-20901
                                                          CIP

| 17 | 16 | 15 | 14 | 13 | 12 | 11 | 10 | 9 | 8 | 7 | 6 | 5 | 4 | 3 | 2 | 1 |
| 04 | 03 | 02 | 01 | 00 | 99 | 98 | 97 | 96 | 95 | 94 | 93 | 92 | 91 | | | |

1
PERSONAL VALUES

Judith Allen Shelly

I 've had it with nursing! I can't afford to quit, but I wish I could!"
Joan unloaded her frustration as she met with two former colleagues
for coffee. "Things are so stressful on the unit, and they require so
much overtime that I don't even want to think about nursing when
I get home. I've canceled all my subscriptions to nursing journals and
don't go to any nursing related meetings unless it's on hospital time.
I'm taking a pottery class, and I joined a garden club. I've got to think
about something else to keep my sanity."

Ruth pondered Joan's comments, "It sounds like we're both experiencing burnout. I really like nursing, but my family is first priority.
Now I'm working two twelve-hour shifts every weekend and get paid

for full-time. It's a pretty good deal, but I'm tired all the time, and I miss going to church on Sundays. I'm thinking of quitting entirely."

Mary Ann was baffled by her friends. "Nursing has always been tough. When I graduated twenty years ago you never heard anyone talk about stress and burnout, but conditions were even *worse* then than they are today. It hasn't been easy, but I've been able to design a rehab unit that really works and it's exciting to see the patients get better. I love my job!"

Assessing Values

What matters to you most of all in life? How does nursing provide a way for you to express and act upon those deeply held values? In what ways are your values challenged or thwarted by your current involvement with nursing? To what extent do your values arise out of a Christian commitment and world view? How have they been shaped by our culture?

Those are tough questions. Joan, Ruth and Mary Ann answered them in different ways. Most of us could not answer clearly without time for deep reflection, but we usually respond to conflicting values from the gut. They gnaw at us, cause pangs of conscience, jabs of guilt and, often, increase the stress in our lives. Values reflect our actual, deeply held beliefs, the things we hold dear to us. Our values determine our attitudes and behavior.

Value Formation

Most Christians assume that their values are Christian, shaped by faith, prayer and Bible study; however, values are really formed by a great number of influences. They are constantly changing, though most of us hesitate to admit it. Diann Uustal, a consultant on nursing ethics and values, says, "Most of us have lost touch with our own valuing process and often unconsciously choose our values by the degree to which we feel we will be accepted."[1] Cultural norms have a strong influence on our values. No one likes to "make waves." Confronting the status quo creates tensions most of us would rather avoid. After all, isn't "peace" a Christian value? If I make enemies by whistle-blowing, won't that hamper my "Christian witness"? It is easy to rationalize our values in spiritual terms in order to feel comfortable.

Cultural norms are so much a part of us that we often do not even see how they conflict with Christian values. For instance, economic prosperity is a primary goal in our culture. Materialism blurs the line between necessity and luxury so that we are convinced that we need higher and higher incomes, and we have very little time or money to give away. Our culture also highly values "rugged individualism" and "the right to privacy," which are not exactly Christian virtues. We have been taught that the ultimate sin is to "make value judgments," and we not only agree but proof-text it from the Bible. We fear being viewed as judgmental. We are also readily drawn into our culture's plausibility structure. Science and technology are the standards for truth and possibility in our age, and few Christians stop to question their authority.

Values are also shaped by family ties and childhood experiences. Most adults will continue to hold the same basic values as their parents.[2] We may not like our parents' attitudes or behavior, but eventually we may end up demonstrating the same values in our own lives and pass them on to our children.

On the other hand, our values may radically change as a moral response to experience. A nurse who is neutral about abortion may suddenly become passionately pro-life after seeing an aborted fetus gasping for breath. Another person, who works with rape victims, may identify strongly with a pregnant woman's "right to choose." A short-term mission experience in a famine-ravaged land may implant deep values of compassion for the starving and a rejection of Western consumerism. Whereas, a person living in an area where land is fertile and available may respond as an older woman in my community who says, "I think those people in Ethiopia are just lazy. Why don't they plant a little garden like we do?"

Experiences over a lifetime cause our values to shift, weaken or strengthen, change and mature. We begin to see more than one side to value-laden issues. We see cause-and-effect relationships when values are compromised or misplaced. A constant sense of powerlessness in the face of injustice may cause us to value escape over change, resulting in apathy. We may grow tired of fighting and quit the frustrating job, or even leave nursing entirely. On the contrary, we may gain power to act on our values. Education, experience or just plain perseverance may provide opportunities to influence professional and community values.

Group values change over time just as personal values do. A nursing ethics text published in 1923 lauded the values of duty, obedience and credulity (gullibility).[3] Today's nursing literature places a higher value on rights, autonomy and accountability. The influences of a world war when women entered the work force in large numbers, the women's movement and higher educational standards have changed the values of the nursing profession. The "good old fashioned values" were not necessarily better or worse, but they were shaped by different cultural influences. Even in the Bible we see values changing in response to God's involvement with his people. It was only after being in exile and suffering injustice as slaves that the Israelites could see positive value in suffering.[4] Prior to their own experience of suffering, it was viewed only as a sign of God's disfavor and rejection.

Economics also play a large part in values formation. The fact that we are a wealthy nation colors our whole way of thinking. We measure (and value) time by how much it costs. I remember sitting once in a pediatrician's office for an hour and a half while seemingly dozens of children were "worked in" before my daughter's checkup. I grew increasingly angry as I thought about how the physician was collecting thirty-five dollars for each extra appointment, while I had sat and waited after having taken time off from work. In another culture that time might have been viewed as a wonderful opportunity to rest from hard labor and socialize with others who were waiting.

Consider other ways economics affect our values. We throw away mountains of trash, including food, clothing, paper and medical supplies that a poorer country would treasure. We shop impulsively. Shopping is one of the most popular recreational activities in North America. We function according to the values of our employers, rather than our own convictions, to protect our job security. We measure our worth by how much money we make. We jeopardize our mental and physical health, as well as the stability of our families, to work long hours for financial rewards.

Several years ago a nursing colleague told me, "It's been hard for my husband and me to get to church lately because we are both working two jobs, but we have some things that our family thinks are valuable enough to work for, like sending our children to private schools." That couple is now divorced and the children are doing poorly in school because of the family upheaval. Economic values are so strong in our culture that my friend would have been appalled to think that there was any conflict between her values and her commitment to Jesus Christ.

Values and Education
Another major influence on values is our educational system. Education shapes our values more than we would like to admit. Both students and faculty can be so intent on fitting in with the system and the accepted philosophies of academe, that Christian values may be squelched or ignored. For instance, how carefully have you questioned the nursing theories or models of human nature taught in your school of nursing? The world views expressed in some of them are humanistic or even overtly pantheistic. The values they embody can lead to practices that are distinctly anti-Christian. Consider the follow-

ing excerpt from a recent nursing text:

> Spiritual support for the dying and their families should never presume either a belief or the need for one. If faith, which is after all a gift, is not there, we should not impose it, and we should never make patients feel guilty for not having it. The ideal is for us to have our own spirituality integrated into all we do and think. Our own faith should be there without words.[5]

Even the language in this statement is value-laden. The author seems to assume that communicating any spiritual hope apart from what the patient already has would be coercive and guilt producing. While some Christian nurses might object to this statement in principle, they function as if it were true. I have heard many Christian nurses express the same philosophy, rationalizing that they cannot be overtly Christian in a pluralistic setting. The author continues later in the text:

> And since spiritual care-giving transcends religious orientations, personalities, and professional turf, we must all find the common human base of our religious orientations—our "natural religion"—in order to relate it to the needs of others. We must remember that no one is the possessor of *the truth* and everyone has a right to be understood. (pp. 151-52)

This argument for outright paganism almost sounds plausible to our culturally conditioned ears. We fear offending our colleagues and clients by openly discussing the gospel, yet consider the words of Jesus:

> I am the way and the truth and the life. No one comes to the Father except through me. (Jn 14:6)

Add to them the words of Paul:

> In the presence of God and of Christ Jesus, who will judge the living and the dead, and in view of his appearing and his kingdom, I give you this charge: Preach the Word; be prepared in season and out of season; correct, rebuke, and encourage—with great patience and careful instruction. (2 Tim 4:1-2)

Christian Values in a Pluralistic World

I don't think Paul meant for Timothy, or for us, to limit those activities to Sunday mornings or the secure confines of a Bible study group. If we truly believe the gospel and our values arise from faith in Jesus Christ, then we must communicate what we believe and try to infuse nursing with Christian values.

Granted, we must speak in words our colleagues and patients understand, but in so doing we must be careful to use the gospel as our frame of reference, rather than allowing secular nursing to set the agenda and standard. Lesslie Newbigin, former Bishop of the Church of South India, says it well:

> As people who are part of modern Western culture, with its confidence in the validity of its scientific methods, how can we move from the place where we explain the gospel in terms of our modern scientific world-view to the place where we explain our modern scientific world-view from the view of the gospel?[6]

As Christians who are part of the "now and not yet" kingdom of God, we need not be intimidated by the apparent authorities of the world. We are servants of a higher Authority, whom we know as Truth. Yet we are also human beings who live in this world and are shaped by our culture. How can we move out of this moral confusion and clarify our values to the point that we are choosing to live according to biblical values and a truly Christian world view? The apostle Paul provides some guidelines:

> Therefore, I urge you, brothers, in view of God's mercy, to offer your bodies as living sacrifices, holy and pleasing to God—this is your spiritual act of worship. Do not conform any longer to the pattern of this world, but be transformed by the renewing of your mind. Then you will be able to test and approve what God's will is—his good, pleasing and perfect will. (Rom 12:1-2)

First of all, we need to recognize that the basis for our values and ethical conduct is not some rigid moral code we must follow in order to win God's approval. It is "God's mercy." In other words, it is what God has done for us in Jesus Christ and continues to do on a daily basis. God's love constantly poured out upon us demands a response. God is not saying, "Hey, I'm your Father, so you'd better do what I say, or else!" He is asking us to love him and offer ourselves to him in return. That is what being a "living sacrifice" means. A sacrifice is something offered completely to God for his use.

By being a living sacrifice we live in constant relationship to God. The more we nurture that relationship, the more our lives will reflect his values. Prayer, Bible study and Christian fellowship are only the beginning of that nurturing process. They lay the foundation, but the actual relationship is worked out though acting on what you learn.

The Bible often uses the analogy of a marriage to describe God's relationship with us. While communication is extremely important in a marriage, it would not be a true union if the husband and wife merely sat around having intellectual discussions. Instead, marriage involves physical, emotional and spiritual intimacy. It requires the daily working through of schedules, being considerate of one another, enjoying each other, getting along with the extended family and giving up personal goals for each other. It is putting each other first, learning to trust each other and sharing all dimensions of life. In a good marriage the couple will increasingly share each other's values and build their life together upon them. So it is in our relationship with God. We take the values we learn from him into our homes, communities and workplaces and filter all that we see and hear through them.

As we see the world through the eyes of faith, we should be increasingly uncomfortable. It is much easier to be "conformed to this world," or at least pretend that we don't see the values expressed around us. A relationship with Jesus Christ does not allow us to withdraw from the world to seek personal purity or "spirituality," but draws us into active confrontation with the world's values. We are heralds of the kingdom of God—trouble-makers in the world's eyes. Jesus said, "Do not suppose that I have come to bring peace to the earth. I did not come to bring peace, but a sword" (Mt 10:34). The peace comes later (Rev 21:3-5). Right now we are in a battle (1 Pet 4:12; Rev 12:9-12).

That is what it means to be "transformed by the renewing of your mind." It's important for us to "be able to test and approve what God's will is—his good, pleasing and perfect will." As we boldly act on the values the Lord forms in us through prayer, Bible study and interaction with other Christians, we begin to see the power of God displayed. For instance, you may act on faith by getting involved with a sticky situation at work and experience God's faithfulness (though perhaps not in the manner you expected). Through that experience you gain courage to speak up on another issue. Gradually, as you act in obedience to God, not only are you personally transformed, but you will begin to see nursing changed into a profession that reflects God's values. It has happened before in nursing history! Florence Nightingale singlehandedly revolutionized nursing as she fulfilled her "call from God."

Conflicting Values
There is no "Checklist of Christian Values" that you can run down and be assured that you are functioning according to God's will. God gives us many absolutes. The Ten Commandments, Jesus' command to love our neighbors and a priority concern for the poor and disenfranchised are a few. But we live in a complicated society and must learn to exercise discernment. We must continually interpret the situation around us according to God's kingdom values. Our culture and our environment are in constant flux, so different values may take precedence as situations change. God's standards do not change, but the way we live them out may. There are times when quitting a job is the most appropriate response and other times when we must stay

and fight. What is right for one Christian may not be right for another, so we must be careful not to generalize from personal experiences.

Jesus loved the Pharisees and the woman at the well (Jn 4:7ff.) equally. The Pharisees were the respectable leaders of his time, yet he blasted them, calling them "hypocrites," "whitewashed tombs," "serpents" and a "brood of vipers" (Mt 22). That doesn't sound very loving according to our culture's standards—nor his! On the other hand, the woman at the well was the notorious shady lady of the community. Jesus sat down with her, though, asked her for a drink (implying social equality) and quietly discussed her theological and personal concerns. Most of us prefer that image of Jesus.

Most nurses, especially Christian nurses, like to see themselves as gentle, caring people who patiently support and encourage others, but sometimes the value we place on gentleness and patience needs to take second place to assertiveness and justice. That sets us up for conflict and criticism. Jesus faced the same problem. He was never without critics. They finally crucified him. Should we expect any better treatment?

Conflict is painful. It does not feel comfortable. It drains energy, destroys relationships, shatters pride and may cause personal loss. We have been socialized to believe that if we do what is right we will be loved and accepted, so many Christians feel that all conflict is inherently bad and should be avoided.

There have been many times in my life when I have begun to wonder why I always seem to be involved in controversy. Was I really doing God's will, or was I just an ornery person? Such times of personal scrutiny are important. We don't want to get into a "witch-hunt" mentality and generate conflict to gain personal power; however, justice often cannot be won without confrontation.

Jesus calls us to be "salt" and "light" in the world (Mt 5:13-16). Salt when rubbed into a wound causes pain. Light when directed into a dark alley may reveal things we would rather not see. Christian values when advocated and practiced in the kingdom of this world will inevitably cause conflict. To assert that ultimately there is life and hope and truth only through Jesus Christ, or to claim that there are absolute moral standards, is to commit the only real sin in the eyes of many in our culture. Yet, we are called by God to make those value judgments.

The question comes down to whether or not our faith commitment to Jesus Christ is strong enough allow us to leave the comfort of conformity with this world in order to allow God to transform our values. Are we, as nurses, willing to claim and act upon God's values rather than the values of our culture, regardless of the consequences? If so, there is great hope for nursing.

Discussion Questions
Context for Discussion: Romans 12:1-2

   a. What does it mean for you to be a "living sacrifice"?

   b. In what ways are you conformed to this world?

   c. In what ways are you being transformed as a Christian?

   1. Reread the quotes from the nursing text on page 12. What statements can you agree with? Which conflict with Christian belief?

   2. Autonomy is considered a primary value in nursing today. Evaluate the pros and cons of autonomy from a Christian perspective. (See page 156.)

   3. An in-service education program on "Therapeutic Touch" is planned for next week. All nursing personnel are required to attend and participate in the practicum. The director of nursing expects RNs to begin using the technique with patients after the training program. What will you do?

2
A CASE FOR VALUE JUDGMENTS

Arlene B. Miller

Y ou can't force your values on people!"

"You should never make value judgments about your patients!"

These two familiar precepts have long been a part of the wisdom imparted by nursing instructors to students faced with patients whose lifestyles and thinking differ radically from their own. Christian students usually have an added problem dealing with some of their patients whose practices conflict with what they have learned about Christian beliefs, behavior and morality.

I want to argue that the conventional teaching on value judgments is counterproductive and propose another way of relating to persons whose values differ from our own. In the first instance, it is a statement of fact that we cannot force our values on people, for values are derived from a broader view of life and not tagged on piecemeal from without. In the second instance, part of being human is the capacity to value, and we must decide what is valuable. To expect that we should not make value judgments is to expect the impossible.

A case study illustrates the dilemma we face. Rosa M., a twenty-six-year-old woman in active labor, was brought into the emergency department of a local hospital, provoking a heated discussion among the nurses. All the nurses remembered Rosa. She had been admitted previously when she was four months pregnant. She was addicted to heroin and supported her habit through prostitution. She also had AIDS. During her earlier visit she was challenged about her prostitution since she could infect others with the AIDS virus. She replied that she had to support her habit. An appointment was scheduled for an abortion, but she failed to keep it because she "forgot." Now she was headed for the delivery room to give birth to a baby who would be heroin addicted and also have a good chance of being infected with HIV.

"Such people should be shot!" asserted one nurse. If she had been told by her nursing instructor that she was not to make value judgments, she had long since forgotten. I had the distinct impression that everyone else involved in the discussion was also making value judgments—judgments about the woman's right to be living, about her behavior and about her personal worth. She was being judged by a set of criteria upon which most of them agreed. Although I did not agree with all their conclusions, I am glad they were making value judgments. Let me explain why.

Basic to Our Humanity

Valuing is part of being human. It is the essence of nursing. It is fundamental to making ethical decisions. Valuing is integral to the Christian life.

Valuing is basic to our humanity. The Latin root of value is *valere:* to be strong, be of value. Words stemming from this root include valiant, valid, valor and convalesce. Strong values are the basis of thinking, decision making, action and commitment. Godly values are the foundation for caring. Persons who do not care remain uninvolved in life around them, unattached and isolated. Asking nurses not to make value judgments is asking them to deny their capacity for caring. Most often, what they do, I suspect, is to ignore such advice and keep what they are really thinking to themselves. Furthermore, since it is impossible psychologically to avoid making value judgments, such judgments, when unacknowledged, will be expressed covertly to patients through inadequate or impersonal care.

Essential to Nursing

Valuing is essential to nursing. Nursing theories assume certain values. The purpose of nursing theory is to guide nurses in choosing the desirability of one outcome over another. Nurses also use theories to plan care that will enable them to achieve the desired outcome. Without values there would be no theories.

The American Association of Colleges of Nursing curriculum guidelines include seven values essential for the professional nurse: altruism, equality, esthetics, freedom, human dignity, justice and truth.[1] Each of these values is held to shape the attitudes and character of the nurse and to be reflected in specific professional behaviors. Thus far, it seems fair to conclude that we really *do* want to make value judgments.

Basic to Ethical Decision Making

Saying that we should not make value judgments can imply that all values hold equal merit. From an ethical perspective, it is commitment to certain values that both guides us in the decision-making process and motivates us to act on those decisions. If one decision is just as good as another, why bother going through the process of making a decision? Words like *should, ought, good* and *bad* connote value judgments. Surely we do not mean that nurses are not to make ethical decisions!

Finally, we come to religious considerations and specifically Christian concerns. It is religious values that make our colleagues most uncomfortable. I was struck by this recently when I saw a "No Smoking" sign posted on the door of a university professor. The sign carried the name of the American Cancer Society. If it had carried the name of a church, indicating that not smoking was a religious value, would the professor have been considered intrusive for posting his values? But the American Cancer Society gave a scientific endorsement to the admonition that is more acceptable in our culture.

The Importance of Christian Values

The truth is that nurses constantly work within a framework of values. They cannot do otherwise. We teach elderly patients to remove loose throw rugs lest they fall because we value their physical well-being more than fractured bones. We encourage people to reduce the amount of fat in their diets and to get physical exercise because we value healthy hearts and blood vessels. We guide young families in caring for their new infants because we value physically and emotionally healthy children. Because we value life, we do all in our power to prevent adolescents from taking their own lives. The list could go on and on.

It is interesting to note that the further we move from the core of the person's self, the more free we are to teach our values. For example, we readily teach making changes in the environment to promote safety. Until recently, advocating nonsmoking was considered idealistic and nonproductive, probably because many health personnel were themselves smokers. Smoking was viewed as a matter of personal choice. Today, however, we have scientific evidence for the public health dangers of smoking, so antismoking campaigns are now socially acceptable. But when it comes to advising people to change their sexual behavior, nurses are reluctant to discuss their own values, supposedly because it would drive patients away from treatment. Even the problem of AIDS and other sexually transmitted diseases has not significantly changed our culture's attitudes about sexual permissiveness.

Moralizing is considered ineffective, at best, and invasive at worst. At the root of this hesitancy to confront patients about their personal sexual behavior is a fear of imposing our religious (and specifically Christian) values on others. However, rather than cordoning off our Christian values, I believe that they are the umbrella for all our values, including our nursing values. Indeed, Christian values of patience, compassion and hope provide *the* way to relate to persons whose lives are characterized by behavior proscribed in Scripture.

The behavior of the heroin-addicted, HIV-infected, pregnant woman in the earlier situation goes against all the emergency department nurses have been taught about sexual continence, respect for the well-being of other persons and about care for one's own body. They *should* be making value judgments. In fact, doing so with intention will enable them to give better nursing care. However, there are other important values that were missing from their response—such as patience, compassion and hope for change.

Christians usually try to solve the dilemma by separating the person from the behavior, such as "loving the sinner and hating the sin." However, making such a distinction is not as easy as this popular maxim suggests. Legally, a person is judged guilty or not guilty based on behavior. We ordinarily hold people accountable for their actions. Experts in child development insist that children have great difficulty making such distinctions. So do most adults, as evidenced by the terms we apply to people whose behavior runs afoul of the law—thief, embezzler, murderer and so on. In practice, we tend to characterize people by their behavior.

Distinguishing between the sin and the sinner is not so easy psychologically either. Sigmund Freud[2] and William Glasser[3] both assume a concordance between the inner nature or character of persons and their behavior. Freud, of course, starts with who the person is internally and then proceeds to explain the behavior. Glasser, on the other hand, begins with behavior, which he believes determines the nature of the person. Even though Freud's psychoanalytic theory and Glasser's reality therapy are radically different in their starting points and approaches to therapy, both assume a certain unity between the person and behavior. Each asserts that changes can be made in both character and behavior and that a change in one is related to a corresponding change in the other.

Most importantly, Jesus also taught a correspondence between character and behavior and focused on one or the other of them at different times in his teaching. In Matthew 7:15-20 he focused on behavior:

> Watch out for false prophets. They come to you in sheep's clothing, but inwardly they are ferocious wolves. By their fruit you will recognize them. Do people pick grapes from thornbushes, or figs from thistles? Likewise every good tree bears good fruit, but a bad tree bears bad fruit. A good tree cannot bear bad fruit, and a bad tree cannot bear good fruit. Every tree that does not bear good fruit is cut down and thrown into the fire. Thus, by their fruit you will recognize them.

In Matthew 15:16-20 Jesus started with the character, or heart, of the person to explain behavior:

> Don't you see that whatever enters the mouth goes into the stomach and then out of the body? But the things that come out of the mouth come from the heart, and these make a man "unclean." For out of the heart come evil thoughts, murder, adultery, sexual immorality, theft, false testimony, slander. These are the things that make a man "unclean"; but eating with unwashed hands does not

make him "unclean."

In both passages, Jesus makes it quite clear that character and behavior cannot be separated. We are what we do and what we do determines who we are. From a psychological perspective then, both Freud and Glasser make legitimate points that correspond to the teachings of Jesus.

Jesus, however, also taught about judging other persons. The New Testament content related to making judgments is extensive. Various Greek words with different meanings are translated *judge* and *judgment* in the New Testament. The term *krino* is used most often and carries the sense of: call in question, conclude, condemn, damn. *Krino* is used in the following passages:

Do not judge, or you too will be judged. For in the same way you judge others, you will be judged. (Mt 7:1-2)

Stop judging by mere appearances, and make a right judgment. (Jn 7:24)

You judge by human standards; I pass judgment on no one. But if I do judge, my decisions are right, because I am not alone. I stand with the Father, who sent me. (Jn 8:15-16)

Now we know that God's judgment against those who do such things is based on truth. So when you, a mere man, pass judgment on them and yet do the same things, do you think you will escape God's judgment? (Rom 2:2-3)

Therefore judge nothing before the appointed time; wait till the Lord comes. He will bring to light what is hidden in darkness and will expose the motives of men's hearts. (1 Cor 4:5)

Do you not know that the saints will judge the world? And if you are to judge the world, are you not competent to judge trivial cases? Do you know that we will judge angels? How much more the things of this life! (1 Cor 6:2-3)

Several principles about judgment emerge from these passages. First, the criteria for judgment are not to be one's personal taste. Rather, there is a standard for judgment based on truth that applies likewise to the person who does the judging. Furthermore, things are sometimes not what they seem to be, and only God knows inner motives for what appears to be even acceptable behavior. Finally, judging is something that Christians will indeed do, even judging angels.

While the Scripture does equate behavior and character, as we noted above, it also holds out the promise of change. During our earthly lives, the behavior/character equation is not fixed. Both a change of character and of behavior can take place. To judge that a person is unable to change is to judge prematurely, even though the outward behavior violates standards found in the Ten Commandments and the teachings of Jesus. God shows this kind of patience with us (2 Pet 3:9, 15; Rom 2:4). Thus, to judge a person with a sense of finality—to say "she ought to be shot"—is to fix the behavior/character relationship prematurely. We are told to refrain from this kind of judging. Only God knows the end of the story for each person.

Relating to People with Destructive Values
Jesus himself provides the model for relating to persons whose lives are entangled with behavior that violates God's standards. The classic example is the adulterous woman whom the religious teachers were prepared to stone (Jn 8:1-11). When Jesus challenged, "If any one of you is without sin, let him be the first to throw a stone at her" (Jn 8:11), they left, one at a time, until Jesus was there alone with the woman.

> Jesus straightened up and asked her, "Woman, where are they? Has no one condemned you?" "No one, sir," she said. "Then neither do I condemn you," Jesus declared. "Go now and leave your life of sin." (Jn 8:10-11)

Jesus refused to judge her in the final sense, which would have tied her character permanently to her behavior. Rather, he held up hope and commanded her to change her way of living. It is because of this hope that people can change that Christian nurses refrain from judging persons in an eternal sense, fixing the behavior/character relationship. Christian nurses *should* make value judgments about their patients. Indeed we cannot avoid doing so. It is exactly the Christian values of patience and hope for change that allow us to provide nursing care for persons whose way of living makes them ill physically, emotionally and spiritually. Such an approach does not minimize the seriousness with which we view the lifestyle of these patients. The reason is that the criteria for making such value judgments are not ultimately our own personal taste but a transcendent standard by which we, too, are judged. We ourselves are in need of God's patience and renewal.

Therefore, we make informed value judgments carefully and humbly, using the following guidelines:

1. Clarify our own values: What do we really believe is important?

2. Examine the source of those values: Are they based upon transcendent truths of Scripture or merely personal preferences?

3. Adopt God's attitude of patience and hope toward those for whom we care.

4. Respect the client's God-given responsibility for choosing and accepting the consequences of choice.

5. Approach the client as a fellow recipient of God's patience and compassion.

It is impossible to suspend our critical faculties and attempt to "not make value judgments." However, we must be careful to judge fairly, viewing each client with patience and hope. Perhaps, after establishing a climate of trust, we may even be able to share what God's patience and hope have meant in our own lives.

Discussion Questions
Context for Discussion: Hebrews 5:14

a. How are judgment and maturity related?

b. What kind of "solid food" prepares a Christian to make mature judgments?

1. What makes it impossible to refrain from making value judgments?

2. If you had been a nurse in the emergency room scene on page 20, what value judgments would you have made?

3. Describe a situation from your own experience which called for judgment. Review the steps on page 27, and discuss how you could handle the situation constructively.

4. What risk do you take by judging someone? (See Mt 7:1 and Rom 2:1-11.)

5. What qualifications and limits does Jesus set on your ability to judge? (See Mt 7:2-5; Jn 7:24 and 8:15-16.)

6. What attitudes should characterize a Christian's relationship with those judged? (See Rom 12:14-21; Eph 4:31-32; Gal 3:12-14.)

3
ASSESSING YOUR VALUES

Judith Allen Shelly

*C*arrie, who was married and the mother of two young children, often quickly mentioned that she viewed nursing as a ministry. She wanted her nursing care to reflect Jesus Christ. And Carrie was an excellent nurse. Her competence resulted in rapid promotions and many job offers. Eventually, she decided to work two twelve-hour shifts each weekend at a hospital (for which she was paid the same as a forty-hour week) and accept another full-time job in industry. When a sports-nursing position opened at the high school Tuesday and Friday evenings, she accepted that job as well. She explained to her friends at church that she could no longer attend Sunday school and worship because she was working on Sundays. Her children also stopped coming because her husband did not attend. Although she loved nursing, Carrie reluctantly admitted that the extra income was nice too.

Katie viewed herself as a committed Christian. She entered nursing because she wanted to serve God. She was active in her church and easily shared her faith with friends and colleagues. In her senior year of college Katie fell in love with Judd. After graduation she moved in with him. "I know our living situation isn't what some people say is right, but what really counts is that we are faithful to each other, not to society's norms," Katie explained.

Values Clarification

What values actually drove Carrie and Katie? Personal values are not always what they seem to be. What we think we value is not necessarily what we truly value; hence the need for "values clarification."

Values clarification has unjustly received a bad reputation in some Christian circles. Some complain that, although it may help people identify their personal values, it does not provide any guidance toward traditional moral values. Yet, the problem is that most Christians assume that their values are Christian, but in reality they may be far from God's standards. While values clarification alone is not a sufficient system for teaching Christian values, it is a necessary first step.

As we saw in chapter one, our values have been shaped by many environmental influences, not merely our Christian faith. Carrie was strongly influenced by a work ethic she learned from her parents, as well as society's value of wealth as a measure of success. Katie grew up in a permissive environment that valued immediate personal gratification of sexual and other desires. Those values were so strongly ingrained that she did not really think that living with her boyfriend was incompatible with God's standard of chastity.

Unless we clarify our values, we cannot begin to change them to be more consistent with biblical values. The process of valuing involves three major steps: choosing, prizing and acting.[1]

Choosing is the cognitive aspect of valuing. We must choose a value freely from several alternatives after considering the consequences of each. The new value is then fit into an established value system to complement previous values. For the Christian, that involves filtering a value through our understanding of the gospel and basic morality.

For example, choosing to value nursing as a ministry must be placed in the context of seeing life as ministry. Carrie needed to reevaluate her understanding of the value she espoused. Although she provided excellent nursing care, prayed with her patients and taught spiritual care workshops, she was ignoring her family relationships and neglecting her spiritual development. She was also unconsciously becoming more materialistic as her wealth increased.

Prizing is the affective component of valuing. It is feeling good about where you stand and communicating that to others with a sense of confidence. It also involves hearing someone else's position without feeling threatened. A person who is afraid to speak up for a personal value probably does not hold that value as strongly as professed. For example, if your commitment to Jesus Christ is truly a personal value, you can witness to others about your faith. You will not let fear of ridicule or rejection hinder you, because you know that the gospel is truly good news (despite how it is perceived by non-Christians).

Katie was beginning to prize the choice she had made to live with Judd. Her ability to explain her rationale to others without defensiveness showed what she truly valued. Her values even colored her Bible study. She claimed that marriage was a more recent, civil arrangement devised by society. "Real" marriage, she believed, was an agreement between two people sealed by a sexual union. She gleaned that understanding from Old Testament accounts of Abraham, David, Ruth and Boaz. In her mind she and Judd were married. A year later she discovered that Judd did not share that understanding, and the value of legal marriage suddenly increased for her.

Acting is the behavioral response to a value. It involves affirming the value publicly and, then, consistently demonstrating the value in your behavior. You also may have to suffer consequences that result from your actions. For instance, nurses who oppose abortion because they value fetal life have acted on that value. They have established crisis pregnancy centers, cared for women with unplanned pregnancies, adopted babies (including those with special needs), demonstrated at abortion clinics and rallies, and refused to work in hospitals where abortions are performed. The consequences may range from personal inconvenience to serving time in jail, but if the sanctity of life is truly valued, those consequences will not change the value. In fact it is the constant force of opposition that imbeds values deeply into our consciences.

On a more personal level Carrie's increasing value of wealth as a measure of success drove her to act. She worked one part-time and two full-time jobs despite the consequences. Those consequences became especially severe when her husband filed for divorce and attempted to gain custody of the children. She eventually gained full custody but then moved to another area and began working three jobs again, leaving the children in a day-care center.

What do you truly value? How do your choices reflect those values? Are you proud of the choices you have made, and confident that they are right? How do your actions demonstrate your values? In their book *Resident Aliens,* Stanley Hauerwas and William Willimon assert that if we choose values that are truly Christian, they will not make sense to the rest of the world. They claim that the fundamental issue of Christian ethics is "whether we shall be faithful to the church's peculiar vision of what it means to live and act as disciples."[2]

Clarification Worksheet

The following worksheet is a values clarification exercise. Fifty values are listed. They come from nursing literature, past and present, and the teachings of philosophy and religion (both Christian and non-Christian). Read through the entire list first, and then mark in column:

A—the ten values that are *most important to you*. In other words, which values most affect your personal attitudes and behavior.

B—the ten values which *you believe most commonly govern actual nursing practice in your work setting*. This includes hospital policy, priorities set by nursing administration, and actual attitudes and behavior of your colleagues.

C—the values which you believe are *most needed as a corrective to problems in your work setting*. What values would you or others need to act upon to cause change?

D—Mark *all* the values that *you believe are compatible with your religious beliefs. (List ends next page.)*

Note: In columns *A, B* and *C* you choose *ten* values for each column. In column *D* you mark *all* the values that qualify.

	A	B	C	D		A	B	C	D
altruism	□	□	□	□	hope	□	□	□	□
ambition	□	□	□	□	human dignity	□	□	□	□
assertiveness	□	□	□	□	humility	□	□	□	□
authority	□	□	□	□	integrity	□	□	□	□
autonomy	□	□	□	□	interdependence	□	□	□	□
beneficence	□	□	□	□	justice	□	□	□	□
compassion	□	□	□	□	love	□	□	□	□
competence	□	□	□	□	patience	□	□	□	□
confidentiality	□	□	□	□	peace	□	□	□	□
cost effectiveness	□	□	□	□	power	□	□	□	□
courage	□	□	□	□	productivity	□	□	□	□
duty	□	□	□	□	progress	□	□	□	□
education	□	□	□	□	prosperity	□	□	□	□
efficiency	□	□	□	□	quality of life	□	□	□	□
encouragement	□	□	□	□	respect	□	□	□	□
equality	□	□	□	□	sanctity of life	□	□	□	□
esthetics	□	□	□	□	security	□	□	□	□

excellence	☐	☐	☐	☐	self-actualization	☐	☐	☐	☐
faith	☐	☐	☐	☐	serving	☐	☐	☐	☐
fidelity	☐	☐	☐	☐	technology	☐	☐	☐	☐
forgiveness	☐	☐	☐	☐	tolerance	☐	☐	☐	☐
freedom	☐	☐	☐	☐	tradition	☐	☐	☐	☐
group approval	☐	☐	☐	☐	truth	☐	☐	☐	☐
happiness	☐	☐	☐	☐	vengeance	☐	☐	☐	☐
health	☐	☐	☐	☐	wisdom	☐	☐	☐	☐

Scoring the Values Worksheet

1. Count the number of values marked in *column A* that are also marked in *B*: _____ x 10 = _____ %

2. Count the number of values marked in *column A* that are also marked in *D*: _____ x 10 = _____ %

3. Count the number of values marked in *column B* that are also marked in *D*: _____ x 10 = _____ %

4. Count the number of values marked in *column C* that are also marked in D: _____ x 10 = _____ %

Interpreting Your Results

The correlation between column *A* and column *B* (#1) indicates how your personal values compare with the values you encounter on the job. So often, when I use this exercise with groups of nurses, this comparison sparks lively discussion. "So that's why I'm feeling so much stress at work!" is a common expression.

Nursing and health care are in transition. In the process many long-held values are being challenged. Nurses, physicians and hospital administrators in some health care agencies do not share the same values. Christians may find their personal values ridiculed or ignored. Experienced nurses may not share the values of new graduates.

If your score shows a low correlation between personal values and the values you confront in your daily work, you may be feeling discouraged, misunderstood, angry, frustrated or just plain "burned out."

On the other hand, if your values are solidly entrenched and you have a strong support system, you may be feeling a great deal of satisfaction with being able to work for change in a difficult situation.

The best action to take if your score indicates strong value conflicts is to find, or start, a support group of nurses who share your values. Some nurses have found this support through a Bible-study or prayer group which meets over lunch, or just before or after work. Groups of nurses in churches, neighborhoods and metropolitan areas are meeting around the country. Even just one other nurse, with whom you can share and pray, can be a great encouragement. For more information about existing groups or resources to start your own, contact Nurses Christian Fellowship, P.O. Box 7895, Madison, WI 53707.

The correlation between column A and column D (#2) shows how your personal values compare with your religious beliefs. Don't be surprised if the correlation is not 100%. Very few nurses find complete agreement between what they think they believe and what they consider most valuable. The reason for this discrepancy is not necessarily rank hypocrisy. Sometimes the problem is a misconception about what the Bible teaches. For instance, one nursing administrator agonized when she realized that she strongly valued cost effectiveness, but at the same time she did not think it was a Christian value. She remembered Jesus saying, "Do not worry about your life, what you will eat; or about your body, what you will wear" (Lk 12:22). But she forgot that he also said, "Suppose one of you wants to build a tower. Will he not first sit down and estimate the cost to see if he has enough to complete it?" (Lk 14:28). Christians often think that ambition, assertiveness and esthetics are inconsistent with biblical values, but that is not necessarily so. On the other hand, we are human beings, living in a human culture, and we naturally absorb many of our culture's values without questioning. Group approval is probably one of the strongest values in our culture. It may cause us to give less priority to more important ones such as justice, compassion and fidelity.

You may want to study the values that did not match up in columns *A* and *D*. The appendix contains a dictionary of Christian values, providing a biblical-theme study of each value listed. You can also consider how you developed specific values. Did they come from your nursing education? your family? your peer group? your experiences? your studies of Scripture?

The correlation between columns B and D (#3) provides a picture of how you perceive your work environment in relationship to your religious beliefs. A low correlation may suggest a situation that is hostile to Christian faith—or at least that you feel is hostile. Can you function freely as a Christian at work? How do you cope with differences between your beliefs and the values in your work setting?

The first step may be to begin open dialog about your concerns. Sue, a newly graduated staff nurse, was sure that she was the only Christian on her unit. She tried to do the best job she could, expecting to "witness by actions," but never mentioned her faith. She felt fearful and insecure. Six months later she discovered that two other Christian nurses on the unit were meeting daily over lunch to pray.

Bob, on the other hand, met an entirely different situation. He discovered that one of his coworkers was stealing narcotics from the medicine cart. The other staff were aware of the problem, but they were attempting to cover for their colleague. Bob decided he could not enter into the deception, even though it might mean alienating himself from his coworkers. He believed that his faith demanded that he value integrity, justice and truth over group approval, tolerance and confidentiality.

The correlation between column C and column D (#4) shows how we act in difficult situations in comparison to how we think we ought to act, based on our beliefs. The correlation here is usually lower than the correlation between personal values (column A) and religious beliefs. We are a pragmatic culture. If something works, we're inclined to try it, then think about it later.

If your score is not 100 per cent, what accounts for the inconsistency? Again, it might be a misinterpretation of what the Bible teaches. It also might imply that you need to examine the values that shape your behavior when change is needed.

However, this correlation can be deceptive. You could score 100 per cent and still have reason for concern. Most nurses tend to choose the passive values in column C. The top ten values (from highest to lowest) in informal studies using this tool were tolerance, compassion, respect, truth, courage, encouragement, wisdom, education, love, human dignity. Earlier questionnaires also listed being nonjudgmental, open-minded and tolerant, and they were consistently the top three choices in column C. These are all admirable values, which to some extent are consistent with Christian beliefs. However, when the problems in a nursing situation are injustice, incompetence, immorality or maleficence, then tolerance and being nonjudgmental are not appropriate responses.

In this exercise you have measured your perceived values. Your actual values are the ones which govern your behavior in everyday life. The next step in clarifying your values is to evaluate your actions at the end of the day. How did you actually respond to your patients and colleagues? Are the values you marked truly reflected in your behavior? The challenge for you as a Christian is to bring your professed values in line with God's values, and then allow those values to shape your character.

Discussion Questions
Context for Discussion: Psalm 139

a. How can asking God to "search me . . . and know my heart! Test me and know my anxious thoughts!" (v. 23) help you to assess your values?

b. How does it make you feel to know that God knows everything about you?

Questions below relate to your scores on page 34.

1. Compare the values marked in column A with those marked in column B. How do your personal values compare with the ones you encounter in your work situation?

What relationship might there be between the level of correlation between columns A and B and your stress level?

2. How consistent are your personal values (column A) with your religious beliefs (column D)?

If your score is not 100 per cent, what accounts for the difference?

What are the primary influences shaping your personal values?

3. How consistent are the values governing nursing practice in your work setting (column B) with your religious beliefs (column D)? Which values seem most in conflict?

How do you account for the differences between your religious beliefs and the values in your work setting?

4. How consistent are the values you believe are "most needed as a corrective to problems in your work setting" (column C) with your religious beliefs (column D)?

If the score is not 100 per cent, what accounts for the difference?

How can you bring your convictions in column C closer to your beliefs in column D?

4
A HISTORY OF NURSING VALUES
Judith Allen Shelly

Nurses are different. They do not necessarily reflect all of our culture's values. Recent studies show that nurses and nursing students place more value on altruistic and philanthropic services than the general female population.[1] Nursing still attracts idealistic women and men who want to "help other people" and "serve God." We probably owe that debt to Florence Nightingale. But nursing is changing, and so are nursing values.

Changing Values
According to one study, a single year in graduate school caused students to increase significantly in valuing support, recognition and

independence, and decrease in the values of benevolence, conformity and practical mindedness.[2] In turn, those changed values then must face the sometimes conflicting expectations of the "real world" of nursing.[3] The result is overwhelming stress, which again reshapes the nurse's values to match more closely the values of society in general. One nursing educator sees this as a positive development. She says, "In fact, it is a sign of vitality that our profession so sensitively reflects the mood, dilemmas, hopes and forces of the society surrounding us—a society whose core values are in flux."[4]

Reflection of Society's Values

While symbolizing idealistic values, actual nursing practice has always been a fairly close reflection of society's values. Even Charles Dickens's much maligned Sarah Gamp was a product of her time.[5] While Sarah Gamp has been decried over the past hundred years as the ultimate example of what nursing should not be, a closer look shows that she might easily fit into today's professional nursing.

Apart from her alcoholism, Mrs. Gamp was quite a modern, liberated woman. A widow, she lived alone in her apartment. Unfettered by the hospital system, she maintained an independent practice, taking referrals from other nurses, physicians, undertakers and satisfied customers. A shrewd businesswoman, she maintained a close network of professional colleagues and assertively educated the public about her professional services. Her assessment skills were superb. She prided herself on her scientific knowledge. Sarah Gamp maintained a scrupulous sense of confidentiality and professional decorum. She was willing to come to work at any hour and frequently worked a double shift—and each shift was twenty-four hours! She certainly verbalized a deep concern for altruistic and philanthropic services, although personal gain was always a strong motivator.

"What a blessed thing it is to make sick people happy in their beds, and never mind one's self as long as one can do a service!" Sarah

Gamp sighed as she meditated over her mug of gin and warm water while her patient slept (p. 419).

But Sarah's altruism did not stand in the way of participating "in the profession's efforts to establish and maintain conditions of employment conducive to high quality nursing care,"[6] or at least to making conditions conducive to personal satisfaction. She clearly communicated her fee schedule and made sure that the work environment suited her, even if it meant borrowing the patient's pillow to make herself more comfortable. Sarah had her faults, but she probably does not deserve to be censured as the anathema of nursing. She was a cut above the general population of her time. If anything, Sarah Gamp was probably closer to today's average nurse than our heroine, Florence Nightingale.

Confronting the Status Quo

Florence was unique. She did not reflect her society's values. She was willing to confront the status quo with the strength of her convictions. At seventeen she received a call from God for future "service," which changed her life and eventually led her to radically reform the nursing profession.[7] Young women in the 1850s were no more interested in "service" than nurses are today, yet that is how Florence viewed nursing. Her parents objected so strongly that she did not enter nursing until she was thirty-one-years old.[8]

When Florence Nightingale entered nursing, nurses were known for their disreputable behavior. Many of them were prostitutes, thieves and alcoholics. Hospitals were filthy, vermin-filled death traps. Florence not only cleaned up the hospitals, but she insisted that her nurses live virtuous lives. She believed that nursing involved "teaching people how to live,"[9] and to do so, nurses must first be above reproach themselves.

Although Florence Nightingale viewed nursing as "service," she was no mere handmaiden. Her primary concern was the welfare of patients. She dressed wounds and braved cholera wards to care for dying soldiers at the bedside; but she also battled hospital, military and government policy to create change.[10] Her reforms reduced the British death rate in the Crimea from 42.7 per cent to 2.2 per cent within six months.[11] Furthermore, Florence Nightingale's influence was not limited to her immediate situation. She advocated for patients' rights directly to Queen Victoria and Members of Parliament. She used her "network" of acquaintances to submit bills to the British legislature. They were passed. She wrote profusely, doing careful research, so that her reports to the government brought action. In 1860 she established the Nightingale Training School for Nurses, the first organized school of nursing. She wrote the primary textbook, *Notes on Nursing*. Florence Nightingale's influence continued to be the guiding inspiration for nursing in the United States for the next century. The "Nightingale Pledge" became the first widely accepted code for nurses. Although not written by Florence Nightingale, it embodied many of her professional concerns. Based on the Oath of Hippocrates, it was formulated by Mrs. Lystra E. Gretter, and a special committee at the Farrand Training School of Harper Hospital, Detroit, Michigan, in 1893.[12] Reciting the pledge at graduation became an emotionally charged rite-of-passage for nurses until the mid-twentieth century when most schools dropped it because of its "medical model" and "handmaiden" orientation. The pledge encapsulates nursing values in the early- to mid-twentieth century.

The Nightingale Pledge

I solemnly pledge myself before God and in the presence of this assembly:

1. To pass my life in purity and to practice my profession faithfully.

The Nightingale Pledge begins with a twofold accountability, first to God and then to "this assembly." The assembly (usually at a graduation ceremony) included professional colleagues, classmates, undergraduates, teachers, friends and family members. It implied a strong valuing of faith and commitment. Professional nursing in the United States began with a distinctly Christian foundation. Christian virtues were widely taught as the basis for nursing ethics. Even before "holism" became a catchword in nursing, living a virtuous life, both personally and professionally, was stressed in nursing education. Early nursing textbooks devoted huge portions to such topics as "duty," "conduct," "virtues" and "discipline."[13] Some of those virtues, such as "obedience" and "credulity," may sound strange in our modern ears because they conflict with the ultimate value of our society: autonomy.

In professing accountability to God the Nightingale Pledge assumes a higher valuing of obedience to God. Autonomy from God, or from God's justice or compassion, was not an option. Likewise, in pledging before an assembly of colleagues and peers the nurse assumed interdependence. The nurse who subscribed to the pledge stood firmly in a community and a tradition that provided a recognized identity to the public. In reality that often meant a fairly blind obedience to the physician and the hospital hierarchy for nurses in the first half of this century.

Practicing the profession faithfully was a full-time vocation, not merely a job. It meant representing nurses and nursing whenever a nurse spoke in public; recognizing health needs in the community and society, in general, and seeking to meet them; and being loyal to professional colleagues. Again, for most nurses in the early- to mid-twentieth century, reality did not match the ideal. Nurses worked long hours and lived either with the family or at the hospital that employed them. They were not expected to have a social life apart from nursing, and marriage usually ended a nurse's career. The high degree of commitment required of nurses was not necessarily detrimental. Many idealistic young women were drawn to the profession for that very reason.

2. I will abstain from whatever is deleterious and mischievous, and will not take or knowingly administer any harmful drug.

Nonmaleficence may seem like a rather obvious nursing value, but closer examination shows that we are teetering on the brink of ignoring it in many situations. The portion of the Hippocratic Oath on which this section of the pledge is based was more specific. It stated:

> I will neither give a deadly drug to anybody if asked for it, nor will I make a suggestion to this effect. Similarly, I will not give to a woman an abortive remedy. In purity and holiness I will guard my life and my art.

The great concern for life at its beginning and end was not shared by the general population in the fourth century B.C. when the oath was written by a small group of Pythagorean physicians. There were no laws against either suicide or abortion at the time. In fact some groups viewed suicide as a courageous triumph over fate. Abortion was considered essential for a well-ordered state.[14] It was a situation much like our own.

Today, a growing euthanasia movement is working hard to legalize "assisted suicides" and termination of life when the patient wants to die. Some would go as far saying that the family or the physician could decide when to end a life without consulting the patient. Many people in our youth-oriented, pleasure-seeking society see euthanasia as the best solution to human suffering.[15] Others, including the United States government, tout the cost-effectiveness of "Living Wills" and the aborting of unwanted pregnancies.[16] While technology has changed over the years, the means to euthanasia and abortion have always been available.

Nursing has traditionally opposed hastening death in any form. A 1937 nursing text states:

> To deliberately put a child to death is rightly regarded as one of the most dastardly of sins and crimes. How can the fact that the child is unborn, still in utero, make the taking of its life anything but murder?[17]

In stark contrast many professional-nursing organizations today are increasingly advocating a woman's right to have an abortion.[18] While euthanasia continues to be repugnant to most nurses, many are becoming disillusioned with technology which prolongs the dying process, and some have taken steps toward active euthanasia.[19]

Both the Nightingale Pledge and the Hippocratic Oath include the nurse's or physician's personal integrity, as well as their responsibility to the patient. Substance abuse has always been a temptation for health-care personnel. Sarah Gamp "like most persons who have attained to great eminence in their profession, took hers [spirits] very kindly."[20] Today's nurses may be similarly tempted to drug and alcohol abuse, as well as other destructive behavior, but the pledge assumes that nurses must remain above reproach to provide quality nursing care.

3. I will do all in my power to maintain and elevate the standard of my profession . . .

Nursing called itself a "profession" even before the reforms begun by Florence Nightingale. The classic elements of a profession include: (1) the value placed on systematic knowledge (knowing), (2) the value placed on technical skill (doing), and (3) the value placed upon using that knowledge and skill for the benefit of society (serving).[21] Florence Nightingale probably epitomized these values in her understanding of nursing. As nursing's body of knowledge has grown and the number of technical skills needed for proficiency has increased, the value and idea of service has changed as well. Nursing continues to struggle with the balance between knowing, doing and serving. Early twentieth-century nursing focused primarily on service. A 1916 nursing text sums up that concern:

> *The most important thing* for a nurse to examine herself in, when she faces the wide field of nursing, is regarding her own attitude of mind toward nursing, her own ideals of service. Is she conscious of a sincere desire to be broadly helpful in her own sphere, to go where she is needed most, to play well her part in the drama of

life? Does she recognize any obligations of service to humanity because of the opportunity which has been hers to become a skilled workman? Has she adopted for herself any guiding principles which, if followed, will help her to make the most of life and yield the greatest possible sum of happiness to herself and others?

If a nurse desires a life that is abundant, rich, and satisfying, yielding a full measure of happiness, she will find it through service, and in no other way.[22]

Today, the focus has shifted from service to knowledge. Nursing values in the last decade have shifted from "passivity, dependency, action-oriented practicality, and anti-intellectualism" to "independent decision-making functions of nurses, and practice based on nursing science."[23] Research, advanced degrees, scientific nursing theories, nursing diagnosis and creating a nursing taxonomy consume nursing leaders as they seek to upgrade the profession.

Nursing's understanding of service has been reshaped by society's value of consumerism. The "patient" is now a "client," a relationship that implies a new set of obligations. Ethicist Allen Verhey sees this as a dangerous trend. He asserts:

A liberal society can be guilty of trivializing ancient wisdom about human flourishing when it renders the professions . . . merely instrumental skills to satisfy consumer wants.[24]

In the process the understanding of the profession has changed, and public trust has begun to crumble.

. . . and will hold in confidence all personal matters committed to my keeping and all family affairs coming to my knowledge in the practice of my calling.

Confidentiality has always been a strong value in professional nursing. Even Sarah Gamp struggled with the ethical implications of maintaining confidences. Today the issue seems to loom larger as nurses wrestle with their consciences over whether an AIDS patient's spouse or lover should be told the diagnosis against the patient's wish. The limits of confidentiality have grown tighter in recent years. Until fairly recently public health concerns largely outweighed an individual's "right to privacy." The value of confidentiality pertained to the avoidance of gossip but did not include withholding information from professional colleagues or persons whose health and safety were at risk.[25]

4. With loyalty will I endeavor to aid the physician in his work . . .
Perhaps one of the most unquestioned principles of early twentieth century nursing was the nurse's responsibility to follow doctor's orders. Nurses at the turn of the century were expected to give medications but were not allowed to know the names of the medications they dispensed.[26]

But such mindless obedience is not what the pledge professed. Florence Nightingale did not hesitate to question doctor's orders. In fact some doctors grumbled about her power, although they respected her work.[27] The pledge is expressing a commitment to interdependence and colleagueship. Over the years that commitment, for many reasons, has eroded into disrespect and competition between nurses and physicians. That is probably the primary reason that the pledge is seldom used, or even mentioned, in schools of nursing today.

. . . and devote myself to the welfare of those committed to my care.
The final statement in the pledge shows an amazing inclusiveness. *Welfare* is a comprehensive term. It includes the whole person across the health/illness continuum. Florence Nightingale showed her concern for the total welfare of wounded soldiers by initiating legislation to establish recreation rooms in military hospitals. Early nursing pioneers in the United States, such as Lillian Wald, went into settlement houses and private homes to provide health teaching and screening for infants and mothers. Nursing assumes a commitment by the nurse to those in need of health care. Perhaps the pledge was ahead of its time, for while nursing continues to claim "caring" as our primary value, nurse educator Kay Partridge declares:

Patient advocacy always figures prominently on a list of nursing functions. But, unfortunately, our profession does not always carry this stereotype into everyday practice. . . .

What I detect society clamoring for, individual patients longing for, and nursing supposedly focusing on is a patient-centered, humane system of care that places the humanity of us all on the list of standards by which practice will be judged.[28]

Developing a Code for Nursing

The Nightingale Pledge was widely used in North American schools of nursing for the first half of this century, but it never became an officially accepted professional statement. The first actual suggested code was published in the *American Journal of Nursing* in 1926.[29] The code covered the nurse's relationship to the patient, to the physician and other medical professionals, to peers and to the nursing profession. Christian moral values were strongly emphasized, and nurses were urged to practice the "Golden Rule." The nurse was seen as a "citizen" and a "servant." Although the code was studied and discussed, it was never officially adopted.

The first official code was adopted by the American Nurses Association in 1950.[30] While retaining most of the basic points of the earlier code, it had some major differences. The statements about loyalty to the physician and references to values such as "honesty and understanding" were omitted. Revisions were made periodically. By 1969, all references to personal ethics and values were deleted, as were all statements about the physician and other health-care workers. The nurse's responsibility to the patient, society, profession and, also, the importance of research were addressed.[31]

The present Code for Nurses was endorsed by the American Nurses Association in 1976. Most of the statements retained the same principles of earlier codes, but the language was changed to be more inclusive. The term *client* replaced *patient*. The focus moved more clearly toward autonomy, responsibility and accountability of the nurse. Education and research were strongly emphasized in the code and interpretive statements.

The code was again updated in 1985. The revised preamble shows a remarkable return to a basic concern for nursing values and individual virtues. It boldly states:

A code of ethics makes explicit the goals and values of the profession. When individuals become nurses, they make a moral commitment to uphold the values and special moral obligations expressed in their code.

The preamble then lists the "universal moral principles . . . which prescribe and justify nursing actions." They are: respect for persons, autonomy, beneficence, nonmalificence, confidentiality, fidelity and justice.[32]

The present code represents both stability and change in nursing values over the past century. Six of the statements came from the 1926 proposed code and the remainder from the 1960 revision.[33] The values it espouses probably reflect our society's concern for a return to "traditional values." In the sixties and early seventies morality was casual and open to personal interpretation. We are reaping the consequences today. Nursing has joined society in grasping for a value system to undergird our attitudes and behavior.

While the American Nurses Association was awakening to the need to prescribe and justify nursing actions based on moral principles, the American Association of Colleges of Nursing commissioned a panel to define the essential knowledge, practice and *values* that a baccalaureate-nursing graduate should possess. Moving far beyond mere "values clarification," the panel outlined seven "essential values": altruism, equality, esthetics, freedom, human dignity, justice and truth, which are to be "fostered and facilitated by selected educational strategies and the process of socialization into the profession."[34]

At first glance, nursing values today seem to have come full circle with the attitudes and beliefs of Florence Nightingale, but there are some significant differences. First, there has been a major shift from interdependence to autonomy for both the nurse and the patient/client. Second, in our pluralistic society, the source of these "universal" values has been obscured.

The shift from interdependence to autonomy is a mixed blessing. The former nursing practice of following doctors' orders and hospital policy without questioning was degrading and downright dangerous. However, today's militant anti-physician attitude can be equally dangerous. It fosters distrust and competition rather than collaboration. Nurses have demanded equal recognition and authority, but have been unwilling to upgrade minimal educational standards. How can an associate-degree nurse assume equal status with a physician who has a minimum of ten years of post-high school education? But even if they were equal in status, nursing could never be completely autonomous in practice. Nursing and medicine are two different disciplines that must work cooperatively to be effective.

Client autonomy also holds positive and negative implications. While it is extremely important to respect a person's dignity, to enable people to take control of their own health in so much as possible, and to make sure clients are fully informed, there comes a point when a person cannot view health care as just another supermarket. The interpretive statement for Statement One of the 1985 Code makes it clear that "the nurse recognizes those situations in which individual rights to autonomy in health care may temporarily be overridden to preserve the life of the human community." If nurses abdicate the responsibility to act morally and ethically because we assume that the autonomous choices of health-care recipients should take priority, we are violating the higher ethical principle of beneficence (doing good).

Although we may appeal to "traditional values" and "universal moral principles," the understanding and application of those values has varied widely from culture to culture and age to age. What has changed in the last century of nursing is that codes are no longer based on "Christian virtues." Without a clear Christian foundation, nursing has lost its rationale for choosing and defending particular values.

Tradition is not an adequate foundation for values or moral principles. Even an appeal to the classical philosophers does not give us clear ethical principles. Aristotle believed that only mature, upper-class males could achieve "excellence." He excluded women, children, barbarians (non-Greeks), slaves and salaried "mechanics" (manual workers) from his ethical system.[35] Plato's ethical system differed from Aristotle's. Modern philosophers take widely differing positions on ethical issues and principles.

Despite common perception to the contrary, the world's religions do not teach the same basic ethical values. To the Shiite Muslim vengeance is a virtue, but to the Christian it is unacceptable. The Christian concern for the poor and oppressed is not reflected in Hinduism where the Law of Karma determines one's fate. Injustice and suffering can easily be ignored in Hinduism. The Christian maxim of loving our neighbors may seem universal until each religion's understanding of "love" and "neighbor" is unveiled. Even the idea of what is "real" changes from religion to religion. To many Eastern religions the material world is not real, but an illusion, which can be controlled by meditation and concentrated thought. That concept has major implications for physical care in nursing. We are already seeing its impact as New Age religions advocate such modalities as "therapeutic touch," "imaging" and "crystal therapy." After examining the basic values of various belief systems, it is not at all surprising that the nursing profession developed in a Christian milieu. The question is: How long it can survive apart from Christian values? The problem with assuming that we can formulate a mutually agreed-upon professional value system without a Christian world view is that we must discount human nature. The Enlightenment world view and most

Eastern and New Age philosophies see human nature as basically good. Therefore, the autonomous self will make right decisions when a person has enough information. The Christian world view sees human nature as self-centered and morally corrupt, so left to our own devices we make bad choices.

A Biblical Perspective

Romans 1:19-23 (NRSV) tells us:

> . . . what can be known about God is plain to them, because God has shown it to them. Ever since the creation of the world his eternal power and divine nature, invisible though they are, have been understood and seen through the things he has made. So they are without excuse; for though they knew God, they did not honor him as God or gave thanks to him, but they became futile in their thinking, and their senseless minds were darkened. Claiming to be wise, they became fools; and they exchanged the glory of the immortal God for images resembling a mortal human being or birds or four-footed animals or reptiles.

Whenever we attempt to devise a moral system apart from the revealed Word of God, it by nature becomes self-serving and corrupt. We see this in profit-making health-care agencies that refuse to treat the poor, in governments that do not provide access to health care for all citizens and in nurses who refuse to care for people with AIDS. Each of these groups claims moral justification for their policies, but they are still unethical.

The claim to be "Christian" in itself does not assure that values will be pure. Yet, a serious, prayerful study of the Scriptures has historically brought reformation and revitalization to nursing and society. Granted, during some periods of history, Christian fervor has been misdirected, but without the guidance of the Bible and the Holy Spirit the state of health care becomes appalling. Unwanted babies as well as the sick and the dying are left on the street to die. The disabled are locked in dark rooms and treated like animals. It is Jesus Christ who gives us the motivation, the strength and the courage to care.

Discussion Questions

Context for Discussion: John 13:1-17

a. What does Jesus say about the attitude we should have in serving others?

b. In what ways can we "wash feet" in nursing?

1. For what reasons did you go into nursing? How have your reasons for being a nurse changed over the years? What influenced those changes?

2. If you were to reform nursing today, what changes would you make? What are some practical first steps you could take?

3. Read through the ANA *Code for Nurses with Interpretive Statements* (Appendix C). For each statement discuss which values inform the behavior.

Can you fully agree with each statement? If not, which points seem problematic?

5
VALUES IN TODAY'S NURSING
Judith Allen Shelly

*B*arb became a nurse because she wanted to help other people and serve God. She had a strong compassion for sick people. She never really expected to make lots of money, and knew she probably would have to work some evenings and nights. Nursing was a calling that required personal sacrifice, but the satisfaction of doing what she believed God called her to do made up for the disadvantages. Barb is glad she chose nursing. Most of the time she feels satisfied with her career choice.

Yet, Barb's experience at work is not always rosy. Interpersonal conflicts seem to overshadow relationships with other nurses, physicians, other departments, patients, families and management. She also feels stretched to the limits with increased patient acuity and decreased staff. Barb believes that compassion, competence, patience, a strong faith and a good sense of humor are extremely important personal characteristics for survival in nursing. While most of Barb's colleagues share her basic values, they do not hold them quite as strongly. Barb often feels frustrated and alone when she stands up for what she believes is important.

Responses to Survey of Nursing Values
You may identify with "Barb." She is a composite of most of the respondents to the Nurses Christian Fellowship Survey of Nursing Values. In May 1989, 1500 survey forms were sent to a random sampling of *Journal of Christian Nursing* subscribers. All 354 who responded were Christians. Of those, 98 per cent claimed their faith was "extremely" (82 per cent) or "very" (16 per cent) important. Apart from Christian commitment, the demographics represented the general nursing population.[1] The survey results confirmed some hunches, but they also presented some intriguing surprises.

The greatest surprise was the respondents' satisfaction with nursing. Recent media reports describe a serious nursing shortage: bright young women choosing more prestigious careers, few men considering nursing, schools of nursing stepping up recruiting efforts, disgruntled RNs leaving nursing to sell real estate or open boutiques. That may be happening but not among those we surveyed. When asked, "How satisfied do you feel with nursing as a career?" a whopping 89 per cent were satisfied: 31 per cent "love it"; 45 per cent are "usually happy in it"; 13 per cent are "somewhat satisfied." In fact only 1 per cent are ready to quit. That is hardly a mass exodus.

Another pleasant surprise was that most of the values held as "extremely important" by those surveyed were perceived as shared by most of their colleagues. Yet, shared values were not always held with the same degree of conviction by colleagues, which sometimes led to friction between respondents and other nurses. There were also some major differences in several areas that showed the potential for conflict.

Compassion Versus Personal Gratification

For the most part Colleen sensed that the other nurses on her unit shared her compassion for the patients. They offered skilled, competent care and usually took emotional and physical needs into account. But at quitting time all semblance of compassion quickly dissolved. Frequently, an incontinent patient would be left lying in feces while his nurse waited at the time clock for the final minutes of her shift to tick off. At first Colleen would offer to help clean up the patient, but she found that her offer merely created resentment. Her sense of compassion for the patient would not allow her to ignore his situation. She would clean him up herself.

Colleen's extra efforts did not go unnoticed. The patients loved her and usually asked for her to care for them. Her colleagues both admired and resented her. They dubbed her "Super Nurse." Colleen felt a growing sense of bitterness over her colleagues who took advantage of her compassion, but she did not know how to change the situation.

Super Nurse Colleen allowed compassion to govern her nursing practice. Certainly, none of her coworkers would claim to be against compassion, but personal gratification ranked higher in their value system. Our culture has socialized us into valuing self-gratification. Even McDonald's, the wholesome symbol of American values, tells us, "You deserve a break today!" If your shift ends at 3:30 P.M., then you have the right to leave. Why stay around to clean up a mess? You deserve a break! Self-sacrifice and unrewarded acts of compassion, though admired to some extent, are viewed as symptoms of psychological pathology by most people. The survey showed compassion to be "extremely important" to 92 per cent of respondents but only 65 per cent of their colleagues.

Balancing Efficiency and Personal Relationships

Rita also usually stayed late to complete her nursing care. She always seemed disorganized. If a patient needed to talk, Rita took the time to sit at the bedside and listen. She did not want to appear distracted or uninterested. Morning care and scheduled treatments were often pushed aside to deal with problems Rita believed were more important. Yet, Rita's head nurse did not share her sense of priorities. Rita continually received poor evaluations because of her inefficiency.

Although Rita thought efficiency was important, she valued personal relationships more highly. She really wished she could be more efficient, but she wasn't sure whether God cared about efficiency. Her head nurse also valued emotional and spiritual support, but efficiency was something that showed. It could be measured. As she walked through the unit, she became annoyed when she saw unmade beds and unkempt patients. She knew that the supervisor and doctors would soon be making rounds, and she would have to answer for the condition of the unit and the treatments that had not been completed on schedule. Efficiency was rated as "extremely important" to only 56 per cent of respondents, but was perceived to be "extremely important" by 63 per cent in their work settings. It was one of the top ten work values.

Faith As a Value

Tina really liked her coworkers. There was a good sense of teamwork and comradery on her unit, which was known throughout the hospital as an outstanding model of excellent nursing care. But Tina never felt like she completely fit in with the rest of the group. They respected her and worked well with her but often communicated on a personal level by innuendo and lingo that Tina did not understand. After work the whole team, except Tina, went to a nearby bar for a few drinks. As a Christian, Tina felt uncomfortable going to a bar, yet she knew that was where her coworkers' close friendships were being cemented.

Several times she decided to go along and just order a soft drink, but that seemed to make matters worse. They teased her about being a teetotaler, and she cringed at their profanity and stories about their sexual adventures.

Eventually, several of her coworkers came to Tina as a confidant when their personal lives began falling apart. She started a Bible study group with two of those colleagues, and they soon became Christians. Then they began to struggle with the bar scene, which became more and more incompatible with their new values and yet was a way to maintain personal contact with their old friends. Tension also grew on the unit as the bar crowd labeled the Christians as "the holy huddle." On the other hand, they were quick to call on one of their Christian colleagues when a patient seemed in need of spiritual care.

Faith as a value creates an ambivalence in many people. Although most nurses think it is important, they also may see it as an affront to their personal lifestyle. Tina's colleagues deeply respected her Christian commitment. When their superficial lifestyle began to unravel, they came to her for help. At the same time, her refusal to participate in their after-work carousing made them feel guilty and uncomfortable. They turned their discomfort into taunts.

Faith was "extremely important" to 89 per cent of respondents, but seen as governing nursing practice by 52 per cent.

The Importance of Forgiveness
Joann was caught in the middle of an ugly strike situation. Her hospital was clearly being unjust and endangering safe nursing care by its new policies. The union called for a strike. Joann vacillated almost daily in the week before the strike. Although she agreed with the union's position, she felt repulsed by the idea of a strike. She did not think she could walk out on her patients. Joann finally decided to join the strikers, but many of her friends refused.

When the strike was over tensions ran high between the strikers and the "scabs." The strikers were angry with their coworkers who went to work and got paid, weakening their bargaining position, while they sacrificed pay and comfort to picket in the cold and rain. What's more, the strikebreakers were now enjoying the benefits of the strike without working for them. Joann believed that both sides should forgive each other and get back to working together in harmony, but most of her coworkers seemed intent on making life miserable for the strikebreakers.

The idea of forgiveness evokes ambivalent feelings in most people. Joann's coworkers probably would say that vengeance is wrong, but they also would feel justified in their lack of forgiveness for the strikebreakers. Joann's readiness to forgive would be seen as naive and disloyal. The Christian value of forgiveness just doesn't make sense to most people in the heat of day-to-day confrontations. At the same time, people long for forgiveness and reconciliation for past hurts. Forgiveness was viewed as "extremely important" by 82 per cent of respondents, 51 per cent in the nurses' work setting.

The Value of Hope

Bill worked three days a week in a hospital for pay. Then he spent all of his spare time at an inner city clinic as a volunteer. Most of his clinic clients were homeless, substance abusers, and some had AIDS. They were the kind of patients his hospital coworkers tried to avoid. "How can you keep going?" a colleague asked him. "I feel hopeless when I have to care for one patient like that. Yet you go out and look for more."

Bill tried to explain the hope that was in him. It stemmed from his faith in Jesus Christ and his conviction that, in caring for these destitute people, he was caring for Jesus. His colleague just shook his head. That kind of hope was beyond his comprehension.

The value of hope in sustaining life is undisputed. Without hope we are left with despair, unless we choose to live in denial. To a great extent our culture has chosen to deal with its lack of eternal hope through denial. Sources of hope differ widely among people. For nurses, one great source of hope can be found in nursing a patient back to health. When that hope is constantly removed, as it was for Bill's clinic clients, many nurses choose to avoid such work. Bill viewed hope from an eternal perspective, which gave him the encouragement to continue caring for "hopeless" people. Hope was rated "extremely important" by 84 per cent of respondents, 56 per cent in the work setting.

Rating Nursing Values
Most Christian nurses carry a nagging frustration over the discrepancy between Christian values and the values that govern nursing practice in their work settings (see graph A). The differences are not always clear-cut, which adds to the frustration. If you were to list your top ten personal values and ask each of your colleagues if they feel those values are important, most of them would agree with your choices. However, the values that actually govern their behavior may well be very different.

The Nurses Christian Fellowship Survey of Nursing Values consistently found a wide discrepancy between the personal values of Christian nurses responding and the values they perceived as governing nursing practice in their work settings. That discrepancy created constant conflict with their colleagues. When asked to describe the major sources of stress in their work settings, interpersonal conflicts scored the highest (listed by 53 per cent), even higher than work overload (44 per cent). Conflict with other nurses was cited more than twice as often (25 per cent) as conflict with physicians (12 per cent). Interestingly, despite the difference in the strength of commitment to chosen values between those responding and their colleagues, out of the top ten personal values of the respondents, seven were also seen as most important to their coworkers.

GRAPH A

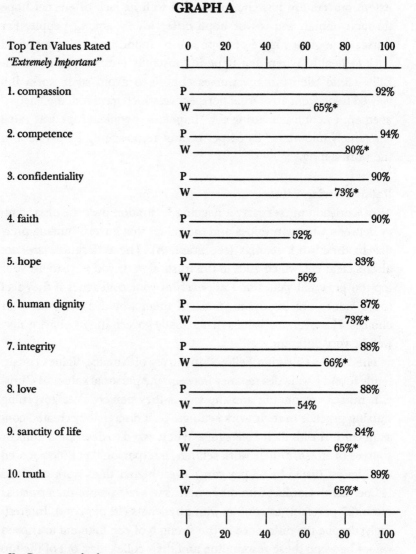

Top Ten Values Rated "Extremely Important"		
	0 20 40 60 80 100	
1. compassion	P	92%
	W	65%*
2. competence	P	94%
	W	80%*
3. confidentiality	P	90%
	W	73%*
4. faith	P	90%
	W	52%
5. hope	P	83%
	W	56%
6. human dignity	P	87%
	W	73%*
7. integrity	P	88%
	W	66%*
8. love	P	88%
	W	54%
9. sanctity of life	P	84%
	W	65%*
10. truth	P	89%
	W	65%*

Key: P = personal value
W = work value (value governing nursing practice in work setting)
* = also rated in top ten of work category

The personal values of those responding closely matched the values they viewed as consistent with their religious beliefs. The high degree of Christian commitment professed by the survey sample and the fact that they were already readers of a journal that integrates Christian faith and nursing show their seriousness about applying Christian values to nursing.

On the other hand, the values they perceived as actually governing nursing practice in their work setting were sometimes in conflict with their Christian beliefs. Nursing is no longer a Christian profession. Not only are nurses themselves becoming more pluralistic, but the very foundation of nursing is shifting from its Christian roots. Nursing theories are increasingly being based on New Age or secular humanistic philosophies.[2] The significant difference between what respondents considered extremely important Christian values and the values in the workplace was consistent with that shift in the philosophical undergirdings of nursing.

Working in a Pluralistic Environment

Nurses who responded to the NCF survey were seriously wrestling with their pluralistic environment. They expressed concern about changing values and questionable practices in their work settings. Many were struggling with ethical problems created by the lack of a common value system and source of authority. They recognized that being a Christian set them apart and deeply affected their nursing care. Several said, "I consider nursing my mission field." Over one-third of the respondents mentioned a desire to serve or please God as one of their primary motivating factors in nursing, but their concerns and approaches varied widely. A few were angry and fearful. They could clearly express their Christian beliefs and moral standards to colleagues but felt that they were in enemy territory. They listed "working with non-Christians" as one of their major stressors. Some expressed contempt for "unrighteous behavior" and "liberal attitudes." Their general response was one of withdrawal and alienation from their colleagues.

Another small number responded with activism. They were concerned with justice and willing to work for it. One nurse said that the opportunity to "help change the system" and "bring my beliefs into reality" motivate her to keep going. While most of the respondents complained about serious problems in their work situation, very few were willing to confront the status quo or stir up controversy.

Most of the nurses responding were neither activists nor isolationists. They quietly went about their work, trying to do the best job possible. One said her motivation comes from "knowing that I am a role model of what a Christian nurse is and that God's standard is excellence." Another summarized the general outlook of most nurses surveyed, "My work is a reflection of my attitude and desire to be a witness for Christ." That witness, for the most part, was silent. Their list of "personal characteristics nurses should have in order to provide good nursing care" (Table III) showed a loving, gentle person with strong faith and personal integrity who gets along well with others and avoids conflict. Most nurses surveyed do not like conflict. About half (45 per cent) avoid it entirely or stay neutral. Most of the rest (43 per cent) try to make peace, viewing themselves as facilitators. Only 6 per cent are willing to take sides.

For well over a decade nurses have been trained and encouraged to be assertive. Yet, assertiveness was at the bottom of the list of ideal personal characteristics, mentioned by only 8 per cent of respondents. In rating assertiveness as a value only 38 per cent believe it is "extremely important." Only 25 per cent think assertiveness is compatible with their religious beliefs.

Donald Posterski, in *Reinventing Evangelism,* concludes that permissiveness is the attitude that controls a pluralistic culture, and tolerance is its golden rule. "In a pluralistic society, a judgmental spirit breaks the social code. Morality is a private matter. Values are sorted according to personal tastes."[3] Most North American Christian nurses have been socialized into a pluralistic mindset. At the same time, we are attempting to apply Christian values to nursing. The quandary leaves us not only morally uncomfortable but ethically paralyzed. Nurse ethicist Mila Ann Aroskar reports, ". . . one still hears arguments that ethical practice is too risky and requires a certain amount of heroism on the part of nurses."[4] Are we ready to be heroes?

Beyond Tolerance
Aroskar goes on to discuss the major influences upon ethical nursing practice. She divides them into "external environments" (clients/patients, other providers, health-care organizations and larger society) and "internal environments of nurses" (mindsets). The mindsets of nurses determine the nature and amount of influence the external environment will have on nursing practice. Her contention is that most nurses allow physicians, the institution or clients to dictate nursing functions; and, therefore, nurses abdicate their responsibility for ethical decision-making. She claims, "It is appalling to discover how frequently nurses are unaware that they are involved in situations requiring consideration of ethical elements." (p. 30)

The idea that there is something that can be identified as ethical nursing practice assumes that there are standards of right and wrong upon which to base decisions. In a pluralistic society those standards are blurred or, sometimes, nonexistent. If the standard is physician's orders, is the nurse being ethical by carrying them out even if they could be harmful? If institutional policy is the standard, does the nurse have any ethical responsibility for patients who are given inadequate care because of their inability to pay? If the client can set the standard, what does the nurse do if the client's demands conflict with professional judgment? Aroskar proposes another mindset that, at first, seems more appealing. She views health care as "the promotion, maintenance and restoration of health within a cooperative community." (p. 24) In this mindset, "all participants' values are taken into account in decision-making processes." The problem here is that all of those values may be different, and some may be diametrically opposed to each other. How is the ultimate decision to be reached? Do the participants vote on the outcome? Is their decision, therefore, ethical?

Ethics was never a democratic process. Ethical decision-making is based on moral values. It is an attempt to determine what is right and wrong, good and bad, and to work toward the best, or perhaps the least bad, solution. When nurses work from an internal environment which is shaped by a Christian world view, their decisions may be different from the majority opinion. The problem is compounded because nursing ethics can never be merely a private matter. Families, clients/patients (present and, perhaps, future) and the entire health team are affected. I cannot make my personal ethical decisions and then let the majority rule, for by doing so I become unethical.

Some Biblical Principles

What then can we do? The example of the apostle Paul in Athens (Acts 17:16ff.) gives some good principles. Athens was a pluralistic society. Its citizens were fascinated by new trends in religion and philosophy. If we were to transplant first-century Athens into the twentieth century, it would probably be the place where new nursing theories would be developed and nursing leaders would gather to exchange ideas. So, what did Paul do?

First, he observed. He noticed the idols. He talked to people in the synagogue and the marketplace and listened to what they were saying. After assessing the situation, he argued with them, presenting an opposing alternative: the gospel of Jesus Christ. The philosophers were both cynical (calling him a "babbler") and intrigued. They brought him to the Areopagus, the center of intellectual ferment, to hear him out. (That was like getting an invitation to New York University to address doctoral students in nursing.)

Again, Paul did a thorough assessment of the situation. He must have spent time observing and listening as well as speaking. He knew enough about his audience to focus on their areas of deepest concern and to commend them for their religious quest. He used their poets and philosophers to prove his argument that Jesus was the one they were actually seeking.

Posterski sums up Paul's approach by saying that he accepted people, appreciated them and influenced them.[5] Paul showed a genuine respect for the Athenian philosophers, though he did not completely agree with them. He met them on their turf and listened to what they had to say before giving his position. He approached them as equals. They must have sensed his acceptance, for then they invited him to tell them more.

Paul also openly appreciated the Athenians. He gave them positive reinforcement for their religious interest and built on that foundation. Rather than saying, "You're all wrong!" he said, "You're on the right track; here's the next step." He showed an understanding and appreciation for their literature, which he had apparently memorized. When he argued his case, he used literature that they viewed as authoritative. He didn't even quote from the Bible (which would have been unfamiliar and probably irrelevant to them).

Paul did not stop with acceptance and appreciation. He didn't present Jesus as just another god to add to the Athenians' pantheon, or himself as a philosopher to stimulate their intellectual curiosity. He made it clear that they had to make a choice. He did not coerce or manipulate. He merely presented his case. Paul did not have 100 per cent success with his audience. Acts 17:32-34 reports that some mocked, others wanted to hear more and some joined him and believed. He was willing to face the scorn of the cynics for the influence he had on others.

Communicating the Good News of Hope

Nursing today is similar to first-century Athens. There is a ferment of intellectual activity as the profession attempts to develop a respectable philosophical foundation. New theories of nursing and conceptual models of the person abound, and they are inherently spiritual, though clothed in secular terminology. Although theories and conceptual models may seem abstract and irrelevant to bedside nurses, they will eventually filter down to the way you practice nursing.

Christian nurses must be willing to enter the marketplace (health-care institutions), religious centers (churches and parachurch organizations), and the Areopagus (universities, nursing organizations and nursing literature) with the gospel of Jesus Christ. We need to accept, appreciate and influence the nursing profession.

The first step is to begin listening seriously and respectfully to our colleagues. What are their concerns, their hopes, their dreams? We need to care about them as people, to enjoy being with them, even if they don't share our faith commitment. We need to discover the things about them that we can truly appreciate and encourage. By doing so we earn the privilege of sharing our own faith perspective and communicating the gospel of Jesus Christ.

Beyond the personal level we need to be informed professionally. Christian nurses should be knowledgeable about nursing trends and their philosophical underpinnings, about nursing theories and about the philosophy of nursing in our own institutions. We should be willing to discuss the implications with our colleagues and supervisors, and express our concerns openly. You may be amazed at the response.

Early in my nursing career, I became annoyed at a newspaper article criticizing nursing. I wrote a letter to the editor describing how I saw nursing as a Christian vocation. In it I quoted from the philosophy of the church-related hospital where I worked. The letter was published and highlighted with a box. The director of nursing made copies of it and posted it on every bulletin board in the hospital. The supervisors discussed the points with staff nurses as they made rounds. There was nothing really profound in that letter to the editor, but because it was printed in the newspaper it became a stimulus for discussion.

Others have had similar results. Nurses who have attended workshops on spiritual care or Christian ethics in nursing have been asked to write articles for the hospital newsletter or conduct in-service programs based on what they learned, often with an enthusiastic response. When Christian nursing instructors have pointed out references to the spiritual realm of nursing in their institutions' philosophies and its absence in the curriculum, they have often been given wide liberties to include spiritual care in the curriculum.

Most nurses are intrinsically religious. The current fascination with New Age and holistic health is an outgrowth of spiritual hunger. Anyone who deals with life, death, suffering and pain has to ask basic questions about meaning, purpose and hope. Many nurses are also hurting people who need the care and compassion of a friend who will help them find answers to their questions and healing for their wounds. If we are willing to accept them as they are and affirm what is good in them, we will have great opportunities to influence both individuals and the nursing profession with the good news of Jesus. The road, though, will not necessarily be smooth. Some will mock. Some will want to hear more. Some will join us and believe. While we must expect the mocking, it is a small price to pay for significant Christian influence.

Effecting Change

Although nurses have considered themselves "change agents" for years, the changes have come more from the external environment (government and institutional policy, fiscal considerations, the women's movement, educational trends) than from the initiative of nurses.

For all the talk about power in nursing, nurses continue to fear power and avoid it whenever possible. Power was rated "extremely important" by only 10 per cent of those surveyed. Another 24 per cent felt it was mildly important. An amazing 23 per cent strongly rejected power. The positive perception of power increased significantly as educational levels increased.[6] Nurses with master's degrees also viewed ambition more positively.[7]

"Power is the ability to influence the behavior of another person; it is the ability or willingness to affect the behavior of others."[8] Power is a necessary ingredient in nursing. The ANA defines nursing as

a direct service, goal oriented, and adaptable to the needs of the individual, the family, and the community during health and illness.[9]

The International Council of Nurses states:

The unique function of the nurse is to assist the individual, sick or well, in the performance of those activities contributing to health or its recovery (or to a peaceful death) that he would perform unaided if he had the necessary strength, will or knowledge.[10]

Nursing requires power.

Power is the ability to act and accomplish goals and objectives. It is a continuous, dynamic mutual process for goal accomplishment and change.[11]

When nurses do not exercise power, we allow the external environment to control us. Perhaps the strong negative view of power among surveyed nurses comes from the perception that power is something other people hold over us. Have we given away our power? In some cases the answer is yes. Christian nurses, especially, have been afraid to use the power God has given us, but there are clear signs of hope for change.

We need not fear power. It is a sign of God's presence. Just before his resurrection, Jesus told his disciples, "I am going to send you what my Father has promised; but stay in the city until you have been clothed with power from on high" (Lk 24:49). Again Jesus told them, "But you will receive power when the Holy Spirit comes on you . . ." (Acts 1:8a). The prophet Isaiah said, "He gives strength to the weary and increases the power of the weak" (Is 40:29). Power is a gift from God that we must exercise responsibly. It is also something we should seek. The apostle Paul prayed for the Colossian Christians and referred to "being strengthened with all power according to his glorious might . . ." (Col 1:11a). Jesus said, ". . . some who are standing here will not taste death before they see the kingdom of God come with power" (Mk 9:1).

Despite the clear case for power as an attribute of God, which he delegates to his people, we fear power for two main reasons. First, most nurses see power abused and are repulsed by its ugliness. Secondly, the exercise of power (even legitimate power) inevitably leads to opposition and conflict.

God intends for us to exercise power for good, to glorify him (Deut 8:17-18; Zech 4:6; 2 Cor 4:7). Yet, whenever people grab power to achieve personal gain, it becomes ugly and sinister. When reputations are slandered, or people are manipulated and injustice is rampant, the natural tendency of most Christians is to pull back from the situation and refuse to get involved. Yet it is specifically in those situations that God calls us to use the power he bestows (Is 58:9b-11; Amos 5:14-15).

Inevitably, the use of power will lead us into confrontation and conflict. Jesus, his disciples, and almost all the early church leaders faced opposition and conflict (e.g., Mt 10:1, 16-25; Jn 10:31-33; Acts 6:8-15; 2 Cor 4:8-12). In most situations that conflict is a lonely battle with very little human support, even from other Christians. It may lead to legal action. It might damage your reputation or at least your relationships.

For example, when Sarah privately confronted Ellen, a colleague, about some blatantly unethical behavior, Ellen quickly began spreading rumors that Sarah was the one who was unethical. Ellen was a convincing liar, and even Sarah's closest friends began to believe Ellen. It took years to restore some of those friendships, and many scars remain. Yet, if Sarah had not confronted, reported and documented Ellen's unethical behavior, many more people could have been seriously hurt, and the reputation of the agency where they worked would have suffered.

The power that God gives us is not necessarily what you would expect. Consider Jesus, who in Luke 4 ". . . returned to Galilee in the power of the Spirit" (v.14). At first people marveled at his teaching. Then, after hearing more, they got angry and attempted to throw him off a cliff. Jesus just walked away and went on teaching, healing and casting out demons. The temptation for us is to believe that God's power will protect us from personal pain and suffering. It won't. Whenever you confront the powers of evil, you will be personally attacked in return. That is a diversionary tactic of the enemy. Once you become embroiled in a battle to preserve your personal reputation, there is no energy left over to fight the real battles. The Lord will eventually vindicate his people (Ps 135:14; Lk 18:1-8). Meanwhile, we must learn to pass through the midst of false accusers, as Jesus did (Lk 4:30), and go on about our business of loving mercy, acting justly and walking humbly with our God (Mi 6:8).

Whenever the New Testament Epistles write about exposing evil and confronting injustice, they quickly turn to the importance of encouraging one another (Rom 1; Eph 5—6; 1 Thess 5; Heb 10). God does not expect us single-handedly to change the world, or even our own little worlds. His power is poured out on the church, and he intends for us to be in close fellowship with other Christians always but especially when we are in the thick of a spiritual power struggle. The encouragement of other Christians refreshes us, heals our battle wounds and restores our perspective. If we are to walk in the power of God, we also must practice giving and receiving encouragement.

Powers Influencing Nursing Today

Nursing today is under the influence of many powers. Some nursing leaders are intent on personal power and prestige. Some are advocating New Age philosophies and the power of the occult. Some seek power for women over men or nurses over other health-care professionals. We cannot shrink from exercising the power of the kingdom of God to influence nursing for Jesus Christ. Mary Mallison, editor of the *American Journal of Nursing* and a Christian, writes:

> What is it about you—a nurse—that makes you so needed, so indispensable to rural Iowa as to downtown Newark? In part it is because you can imagine the future. And because you can "see" the future, you take steps to alter it.[12]

Altering the Future

How will we alter the future of nursing? Nurses in Korea give us a prime example. When Mo-Im Kim, a nurse with great power and influence in Korea, became president of the Korean Nurses Association she was not a Christian. Christians began to pray for her, and they told her so. In the autumn of 1986 she committed her life to Christ. A Christian friend remarked about Mo-Im Kim: "She has changed so much . . . Now it's as if when she opens her mouth, God comes out."[13] As chairman of the Organizing Committee in Korea that prepared and conducted the International Congress of Nurses in June 1989, Dr. Kim stated:

> We cannot deny that this ICN is an opportunity given by God and Korean nurses need to consider what is God's will for allowing this Congress to be held in Seoul. We must commit ourselves to Him so that He can use us. Each one of us will need to work according to our gifts and talents. In that way we can serve Him so that this Congress will glorify the Creator God in both its order and harmony.[14]

Those who attended the Congress remarked about its unusual spirit of peace and love. Mo-Im Kim was elected president of the International

Council of Nurses. She chose *love* as the watchword for nursing for the next four years. In her first press conference, she declared, "I myself am a Christian nurse."[15] Mo-Im Kim is determined to use her power to influence nursing for Jesus Christ.

In a changing profession with shifting values, it is easy to retreat into feelings of powerlessness. God does not give us that option. We can operate in the power of the Spirit, first, by praying for those in power and joining with other Christians for strength and encouragement; then, by entering the professional arena to exert influence where God has placed us. It may be in one-to-one relationships with patients and colleagues, or it could be on hospital committees, in professional organizations, through professional writing or in positions of leadership. The Holy Spirit has come upon us. We have received power. It is time to stop gazing into heaven and get on with kingdom business.

Discussion Questions
Context for Discussion: Matthew 10:16-39

a. How have you experienced being a "sheep" in the midst of "wolves"?

b. What values does Jesus expect us to hold most important in the face of conflict?

1. What are the problems you most often face in nursing which create stress for you?

2. What motivates you to perform your work in such difficult situations?

3. What personal characteristics do you think nurses should have in order to provide good nursing care?

4. What is your usual response to conflict? How would you like to respond?

5. If you were to confront the problems in your nursing situation, what do you think would happen?

6

FOUNDATIONS FOR CHRISTIAN VALUES

Arlene B. Miller

J ust mention the subject of values around nurses and most of them will immediately begin offering opinions and describing situations where values created dilemmas. What fires this response?

First, nurses are surrounded by complex issues brought on by scientific advancements and technology in health care. Second, society's values are changing rapidly, and nursing feels the need to keep pace and be realistic in its values. A third reason for the interest in values grows out of the need for a united professional voice for influencing public policy in the area of health care. Finally, nursing educators want nursing students to be socialized into the values of the profession.

The so-called ethical dimension in nursing textbooks commonly includes discussions of medical technology, death and dying, sexuality and distribution of health care. More sophisticated nursing ethics courses include an introduction to the field of philosophical ethics and the ethical principles that have traditionally guided health care. Increasingly, clinical discussions for nursing students address ethical and legal questions. Nurses must identify what actions would come from their personal values as they engage in moral and ethical reflection. Diann Uustal writes, "The crucial question is 'Are my values ethical?' " Answering she says, "[this question] demands personal introspection, reflection, and answering by each of us as a nurse before we take action based on personal or professional values."[1]

How do we decide if our values are ethical? Most nurses simply don't know. We are facing a crisis of values both in society and in nursing. Nursing education is increasingly concerned about values and ethics. Yet, when specific nursing values are proclaimed, the foundation on which they rest is left undefined. To the question "Are these values ethical?" there is no commonly agreed upon way to test them. Legal, social, traditional and professional values are some of the standards offered for assessing nursing values.

Legal Standards
In a litigious society nurses are increasingly aware of legal implications of their work. While matters of legality and moral values are related and overlap, most of us intuitively shrink from equating them. For example, nurses complain of the mountains of documentation required to protect themselves and their institutions from being sued. We also see the increasing number of expensive diagnostic procedures that physicians order to protect themselves legally. In following the law to the letter we do not become more ethical. Or, consider government policy and laws that fail to provide adequate health care for the poor. They do not make the neglect moral. On the other hand, should it become legal to help dying patients commit suicide, would

that then be moral for nurses? Even now some nurses working with AIDS patients struggle with the question.

Laws themselves reflect an underlying system of values. Indeed, laws reflect conflicting values, such as the individual's legal right to privacy and society's right to know the emotional stability of its public employees. Yet, an action that is legally permissible may not represent a value that is morally acceptable. The extreme example of recent history comes from Nazi Germany. A value of racial purity was expressed in laws forbidding marriage between Aryans and non-Aryans. A legal killing of millions was justified by such values.

Social Values

If legal standards are inadequate, what about societal values, the so-called community standards? We have already noted that the values of our society are rapidly changing. The only clearly unacceptable position is to claim that there is a universal standard for morality. Even as Christians, we are strongly influenced by the values of tolerance and pluralism. Our democratic environment makes us lean toward majority opinion as the litmus test for what is right. Most of us grew up pleading our case for personal justice with, "But Mom, everybody else is doing it!"

Psychologist Earl Wilson writes the following about the problem of basing one's values on societal acceptance:

The gay-rights appeal in the battle for the person is an appeal of those in misery who want company. They believe and have demonstrated that there is power in numbers. If thousands believe that the practice of homosexuality is their God-given right then how can they be wrong? The answer—easy! The number of people believing a lie has never been sufficient to turn it into the truth.[2]

Most thinking people would agree with Wilson's conclusion that values cannot rest alone on what most people think. But current thinking on issues that affect nurses and health care should be considered if only, in some instances, to be rejected. Yet, accepting the views of the majority may lead us to immoral values.

Traditional Values

Others look to tradition as a source of values. Gail Davis, writing in *Nursing Outlook,* feels that nursing needs a clearly defined value system to give it direction in political-action efforts. She believes that nursing values can be identified from our social heritage.[3] But there are problems with this approach. In chapter four we saw how nursing values have shifted over the years. Some writers, however, identify constant values: caring, respect for persons, beneficence, nonmaleficence, confidentiality, fidelity and justice. But, even as we use the same or related ideas, the content of these constant values might change. Even if it can be established that there is a constancy of nursing values over the years, is that sufficient reason to accept them all as "good" values? I don't think so. For some time now nursing has wanted to shed many of its traditions. Symbols of the "handmaiden" image, such as the cap, are no longer in vogue. With the symbols, the idea of service is also outmoded, even though serving is an integral dimension of constant "caring." How do we decide which traditional values are worth keeping and which should be jettisoned? That is the question.

Professional Values

Along with the traditional values of nursing, the values defined by nurses as a professional body are also viewed as authoritative. We are called to be loyal to nursing and to help further the growth of the profession. The political process of nursing organizations is seen as authenticating the values put forth by these groups. Enhancing the status of nursing—for the good of the clients, of course—is the basis upon which our professional organizations identify nursing values. But professional values themselves may need to be questioned. Their foundation may not be pure altruism. Sociologists Don Kraybill and Phyllis Good point out that, "There is a widespread tendency for professionals to become so engulfed by their professions that they end up serving it rather than their clients, students, and patients."[4] They further note that Christian professionals must wrestle with the tendency for the profession to become a surrogate church and thus the chief source of values, friends, meaning and purpose.

Moral Crisis

The reality is that no one foundation for values exists that would be acceptable to all nurses. The problem in nursing is only a reflection of a much larger societal crisis. Ethicist Lewis B. Smedes writes:

It is a truism today that we are in a crisis of morals. The crisis is not simply that people are doing the wrong things; that has been going on since the Fall in Eden. The crisis is the loss of a shared understanding of what is right. Worse, it is a crisis of doubt as to whether there even is a moral right or wrong at all. The most obvious and sensational evidence of the crisis is in sex and marriage, but it reaches almost every other arena of life as well.[5]

Our society is secular, meaning that in public life we do not have an official national religion. Religion is confined to the private areas of our lives. Our society is also pluralistic. People may espouse any or no religion. Many different religious traditions are present. Pluralism is an American value!

The truth of the matter is that values never exist in isolation. Our values are embedded in our overall view of life and its meaning. A popular term in nursing literature is *value systems*. A value system is the way we rank our values. We make decisions based on the relative importance of one value over another in our system of values.[6]

Religions provide just such a system of values. Ethicist H. Tristram Engelhardt asserts that full-fledged moralities are imbedded in particular traditions (such as Judeo-Christian, Buddhist, Marxist, etc.). He says that they cannot be divorced from those frameworks without distortion.[7] Psychologist Seymour Sarason says that there was a time in Western society when the public interest was defined in religious terms as a relationship between the individual, the group and a divinity. He laments that since the divine has been jettisoned from public life, "No adequate substitute for that triad has been found."[8] We lack a compelling religious center for commonly defined values. This has led to a shifting away from speaking of sin (transgression against divine law) to speaking instead of secular morals and values. Impersonal abstractions, such as public welfare or freedom, are held up as a basis for social values. They are poor substitutes, though, for a personal God. Lacking a commonly accepted authority, each individual is left to find a personal authority.

For nurses who are deeply committed to Jesus Christ the moral crisis in public life is more than an academic discussion. Jesus calls us to bring our total lives, including our nursing, into conformity with his values. Let us now turn to our own tradition. What are "Christian" values, and on what do they rest? Where do we find them?

Christian Values

Christians believe that moral values are rooted in the character of God himself. Philosophers have long debated which is first: moral laws to which God himself is subject, or God who has arbitrarily decreed certain commandments. Each of these views misses the biblical understanding that God *is* good and that from his personal being flows the absolute standard of righteousness for human life. God's goodness is expressed in both his holiness and his love, which lead God to self-sacrifice and the full extension of his favor to his people.[9]

Christians do not begin with discussions about whether God is subject to moral laws or whether supposedly divine moral standards are arbitrary and subject to human evaluation and reformulation. Christians do not start with rules and commandments at all. They start with who God is, the creator and redeemer we come to know through the story of Israel and Jesus. God's character of holiness and love is the foundation for our values and actions.

Having said, though, that God's goodness is the standard for measuring our values, how do we discover what he is like? God has revealed himself to us. He has made his character known. Psalm 19 celebrates the wordless speech of creation. It tells of God's divine power and wisdom and rejoices in the laws and moral principles expressed by God. Theologians refer to these two ways as general revelation, which is generally available, and special revelation, "a particular disclosure about how mankind can find favor with God."[10]

It should not surprise us that even the person who knows little or nothing about the Bible has a sense of right and wrong. God, who is the source of the moral world, created us in his image. All people are like God in that we are moral beings, having an inner moral sense or conscience. This inner moral sense, then, is one aspect of general revelation. Since humans first broke God's law, the human conscience has been flawed. Yet, no one can get rid of the sense that some things are *right,* or *natural,* and others are not. The arguments occur on what actions belong in which categories. The current euthanasia debate provides an example. As public sentiment shifts from protecting life to the "right to die," debate has moved from the injustice of prolonging death to the morality of "aid-in-dying."

Because we live in a moral universe created by God, it is not strange that wise people throughout history have discovered universal-moral principles like justice, benevolence and truth. How often have you cried out in the midst of a frustrating situation, "That's not fair!"? There wasn't time for deep theological reflection. The feeling just came from your gut. Aristotle observed that we know what justice is when we feel the wounds of injustice.[11]

But reflecting upon the natural creation and our own inner moral awareness can leave us with merely a sense of awe and moral perplexity. There is no apparent way to know the meaning of the world and no solution to the moral defects we sense. For example, nurse Margot Fromer describes this frustration:

Theology is the study of God and divine happenings. It is ironic to note that in the end, and always, God remains a mystery, his reasons for doing things unfathomable and unknowable. Yet we continue to speculate about God without ever coming to definitive conclusions. God chooses to remain aloof and unknowable, and he has shown no signs of changing this state of affairs. Theology is fascinating on an intellectual or theoretical level. Other than for speculation as to what God might do next or what he plans for the future of the universe, it seems pointless to debate God's reasons for actions.[12]

But God does not remain in splendid isolation from his creation! He longs to communicate with us and has revealed his thoughts and intentions in ways we can understand. He has done this through his mighty acts, the works he did in human history. He brought his people out of slavery; he sent his Son to live, be crucified and then be raised to life for our salvation. God has also revealed himself by divine speech, through the prophets, culminating in the teaching of Jesus and later the exposition of that teaching by his apostles.[13]

Getting to Know God

God's character is manifested throughout the written record of revelation—the Bible—in the Ten Commandments, the Psalms and Proverbs, the Sermon on the Mount, the ethical teachings of Paul and, ultimately, in the life and death of Jesus Christ.[14] The themes and narratives of the lives of individuals and nations as they either respond to or reject the Lord God bear witness to him. Jesus, the God Man, is the supreme example as he interacts with people in all walks of life—friend and enemy, rich and poor, powerful and powerless, male and female, child and elder, individuals and crowds, neighbor and foreigner. In the Scriptures we learn what God is like, about his holiness and his love, and thus come to know what God values, what is important to him.

At this juncture let us turn to the Bible itself. The idea of value system, to which we referred earlier, will help us here as we consider how the Bible helps us set our values. The Bible is our authority for and the basis upon which we rank our Christian values. Values based on personal preference, law, social consensus, tradition and professional codes may very well fit within the Christian framework. They will always be evaluated and ranked, though, according to our understanding of Scripture.

Also, the Bible provides specific content for what are otherwise abstract ideas. Because of our common humanity and because of the historical Christian influence in shaping our culture's values, many Christian and professional values are similar. The Christian understanding of a particular value, however, may have quite a different meaning from the same value defined in a purely secular sense. For example, the current euthanasia debate presents very different understandings held by modern secularists and by Christians about God's sovereignty and the gift of life, death, the value of suffering and the claims of the community.[15] Ethicist Stanley Hauerwas criticizes modern medical philosophy saying, "The most decisive challenge which medicine raises for Christian convictions and morality involves the attempt to make suffering pointless and thus subject to elimination."[16] Increasingly more people in our society accept suicide or euthanasia as appropriate options in the face of suffering. For the Christian, suffering is not pointless even though it is beyond understanding. Although agonizing, suffering builds character, equips us to care for others. It refines our faith in God, who cares enough to suffer with and for us (Rom 5:3-5; Heb 4:14-16; 1 Pet 4:1).

Think back to Margot Fromer's quote about the futility in trying to find nursing values in theology. She might now be saying, "I told you so!" What does all this have to do with nursing and the realities of poor people unable to pay for health care or short staffing? It is true that the Bible may not specifically address the concerns of modern nurses, but it does give us examples and principles for reflection. We will consider more fully how it applies in chapter nine. For now, though, we can rest assured that God *does* make himself known to us: in creation, in the Bible and, most fully, in the life and teachings of Jesus Christ. From God's character of holiness and love, we can define the foundational values of justice and love. God is the compelling *center* for Christian values.

Discussion Questions
Context for Discussion: Micah 6:8

a. What guidelines does the prophet Micah give for our ethical behavior?

b. How are ethics and faith related?

1. Obtain a copy of the philosophy of your agency or school. What sources seem to provide the foundation for the values expressed?

2. What values do you hold in common with your non-Christian colleagues? What values seem unique to Christian nurses? How do you account for the differences and similarities?

3. Lisa, an RN in the Coronary Care Unit, attended a workshop on "Crystal Therapy" and brought back a supply of crystals which she proceeded to hang in each cubicle. Several of her coworkers complained that the crystals gave them a spooky feeling and wanted them removed. The head nurse finally told Lisa to take the crystals down. Lisa complained, "You say that you want us to meet spiritual needs. What is the difference between my expression of spirituality and your praying with patients?"

a. How would you answer Lisa?

b. On what foundation would you base your answer?

7
NURSING VALUES & CHRISTIAN CHARACTER

Arlene B. Miller

*T*hree West was in its usual hectic state as Eric began his second double-shift of the week. Not only was patient acuity high, but there had also been a constant barrage of interpersonal conflicts among the staff all day. Eric was exhausted and looked forward to going home to relax. But the nursing office called to say that the evening charge nurse and one LPN would not be coming to work. Eric reluctantly agreed to work charge, but no one would fill in for the LPN. As he took stock of the situation he began to wonder if he had made a mistake by staying.

From Bad to Worse

During report Eric became more discouraged. Seven post-ops returned during the day shift—all with IVs and frequent vital sign checks. Two of the IVs had infiltrated and needed to be restarted. Several other people needed special attention. Mr. Jordan in 323, who had a nephrostomy this morning, was particularly unstable. His blood pressure was 70/30. The surgeon had been paged but had not responded yet. Mrs. Miller in 315, a diabetic post-op cholecystectomy, was vomiting and disoriented. The medical resident was with her now. Two more post-ops were still in the recovery room. They would be returning soon. Mrs. Glover in 307 probably would not live through the evening shift. Despite her terminal condition, the physician would not write a "no code" order. Her tearful family stood in the hallway across from her room. They seemed frightened and desperately in need of support. To make matters worse Mrs. Glover was in isolation.

As report continued, an attending physician, well known for his violent temper, stormed into the nurses' station and demanded immediate attention. Eric muttered under his breath, then replied politely, "Your patients are doing well. I'll be with you when I finish report and check on some urgent matters."

The Character of the Nurse

"The person who is the nurse is the critical determinant of the quality of nursing care provided," writes nurse educator Dorothy Reilly. She believes teaching nursing ethics begins with teaching values. In so doing the inner person of the nurse will be changed.[1] Reilly represents a growing group of nurse educators who are concerned with the character of the nurse.

Earlier in nursing history, character building received considerable attention. Until the past few decades nursing education focused on teaching beliefs, values and attitudes. Yet, in today's climate such efforts are usually seen as indoctrination. Further, with the rise of technology and increasing emphasis on skills, concern about nurses' virtues has faded into the background.

Little, if anything, is taught about the character of the nurse in most nursing ethics courses today. Instructors assume that, given the right set of principles and logical skills, nurses will work out ethical responses to complex clinical situations. They focus on duty, codes, decision-making processes and actions in specific cases. Most nurse ethicists work from certain basic principles: justice, beneficence, nonmaleficence, fidelity, veracity and autonomy.[2] These principles are viewed as timeless and universal. Students are given the impression that ethical concerns are primarily those big complex problems caused by technology or life and death situations.

Eric, the harried nurse who opened this chapter, needed more than a set of principles or a decision-making process. The problem he encountered was not one, big critical incident but a jumble of common nursing situations which most nurses face daily. Only the grace of God and the strength of his character would pull him through this shift.

Some ethicists are beginning to question this exclusive focus on duty and decision-making in ethics. One of them is nurse ethicist Marsha Fowler, who writes, "An ethics of duty without regard for the moral character of the agent is an impoverished ethics."[3] The concern for character is central to virtue ethics, which begins with the kind of person who makes moral decisions.

The American Association of Colleges of Nursing's (AACN) National Panel of Essentials of College and University Education for Professional Nursing reflects that concern for character in advocating seven essential values for professional nursing practice.[4] Listed with each value are examples of related attitudes, personal qualities and some professional behaviors which express those characteristics (see appendix D). While the document does not refer to the attitudes and personal qualities as virtues, that is what they are—character traits of the morally excellent nurse. So once again nurse educators are recommending character development as an integral part of nursing education. This listing of virtues is more human and less sexist than some traditional nursing virtues like absolute accuracy, womanliness, patriotism, soft hands and resistance to infection.[5] The AACN document states:

> Values, attitudes, personal qualities, and consistent patterns of behavior begin to develop early in life. They are fostered and helped by selected educational strategies and the process of socialization to the profession.[6]

This document reflects the truth that our values influence our behavior and, ultimately, shape our character. The notion of *character* in nursing is essential, not only for ethical actions in nursing care, but also for the renewal of nurses and nursing itself. Why do I say this? Nursing is our calling from God—our *vocation*. Society values self-fulfillment, but our first loyalty is to Christ and to those whom he gives us to serve in our families and world. Self-fulfillment is not the primary goal. It is rather a kind of benefit or a gift of grace along the way. Often the road to self-fulfillment is paved with suffering and self-denial.

Our values are being formed within that calling as we struggle with the hardships and rejoice in the satisfactions of nursing. Values are those "beliefs or ideals to which an individual is committed and which guide behavior" (see appendix D). You will remember that "valuing" means choosing, prizing and acting. But the "I" that chooses, prizes and acts is not some part of the self that remains untouched by its actions as if it were a conduit for something else. The "I" is *myself*. It is my character. It is who I am. Thus, my values shape who "I" am. They form my character. They determine my very ability to choose, prize and act. As I appropriate Christlike values to guide my behavior, they become *my* attitudes and *my* disposition.

We do not, however, have total autonomy in creating ourselves. Much is already given to us: our social context, our parents and family, our genes and our culture. God has created us each for a purpose, and he is deeply involved in the direction of our lives. Yet, we do have choices. We can choose to be the people God has created us to be, or we can choose to reject him and his direction. We can choose to be moral in tough situations.

Sometimes our situations make that choice seem impossible. Can we be moral in a bureaucratic institution where economics determine staffing and a hierarchy determines policy?[7] In such a setting how can we accept responsibility for our character? How can we survive in the system if we choose values that are not compatible with those of the institution?

Nurses agonize over the lack of respect given them by physicians and administration, and their lack of ability to control their professional practice. It is easy to understand why nurses consider themselves victimized and oppressed. Consider Eric's situation. How could he provide quality whole-person care to the patients on his chaotic unit? The paperwork alone could consume all his time, but he also had an emergency on his hands, a barrage of routine physical tasks, an irate physician pacing the nurses' station and a patient's family who needed support.

It is no surprise that much of the rhetoric coming from nurses is a call for power and release from oppression. How can we claim that nurses are responsible for who they are? Largely, "who we are" has already been defined for us by those in power.

Virtue Ethics
Traditional nursing ethics stresses the importance of responsibility and freedom to make decisions and act. Yet, there are times when we cannot "act" in the immediate situation. Eric could not possibly personally attend to all the needs he observed on his unit. He would have to make choices, but not all of them would be adequate. Virtue ethics provide an alternative, saying that whether I have the power to control

is not as important as realizing that I have the resources I need to deal with situations as they come into my life. Hauerwas refers to this as "making my life my own."[8] Making life mine does not mean that I have the power to choose what happens to me—whether through my decisions, the decisions "they" make or, even, natural events of cause and effect. Rather, writes Hauerwas, "My act is not something I cause, as though it were external to me, but it is mine because I am able to 'fit' it into my ongoing story."[9] I have a history—a past—and what is now occurring in my life is part of "who I am" as I include it in my story.

Thinking of life as an ongoing story, we can either view it as something we create on our own, or we can see it as part of a much larger story that God is writing and directing. We are not given a prepared script. Instead, God invites us to participate actively in the story of his people. We are part of an adventure.

So, how does thinking of my life as a story help the nurse who is feeling pressured by a heavy workload, conflicts with colleagues and ethical dilemmas? It all depends on the nature of the story we tell ourselves. Is the narrative *true*? Does the narrative include God and his mighty acts of creation and redemption as well as human responsibility? Does it account for suffering and death as well as life and joy? Does it recognize both human goodness and perversity? Does it allow for the stories of the people around us: our families, our colleagues, our neighbors? Our personal stories develop within a community that also has a story. Just as the Israelites recounted the mighty works of God whenever they got into tight situations, so we can place our dilemmas into the history of God's faithfulness in our lives.

Back to our pressured nurse. Eric will probably go home feeling exhausted and defeated after his shift today, but he can gain new perspective as he examines the day in the light of his relationship to God. The Christian story—the continuing history of God's people responding to his grace—is a truthful narrative. It accounts for all the complexities and the blessings and pain of human life. Eric can claim his day, confused and painful, as part of this true story. Doing so requires knowing the story and its meaning. It also requires the virtue of courage to act "as if" it is true, even when we do not feel like it.

Developing Christian Character

Specifically, as Eric fits into the Christian narrative he may need to take a moment to quiet himself, take a deep breath and send a prayer to God for help. He can then spend time after the shift reflecting on what happened. He can share and pray with other nurses about how to respond to the physician's insults with a sense of personal dignity. Fitting into the Christian story may lead him to positive acts of compassion for hostile fellow workers. It may mean imitating the confidence of Christ in preparing a list of suggested changes to present to his supervisor. Mostly, it means that he will not succumb to the hopelessness that pervades in the climate of the unit, but instead look with eyes of hope because he serves the God of hope. Eric can respond in this way because he sees himself, in this place and at this time, as playing a part in God's ongoing involvement with people. He is not alone in creating his story but is engaging in a drama whose director is God himself and whose players include the Christian community. Eric is claiming his life as his own. He is choosing virtues that will develop into Christian character.

Some Christians argue that an emphasis on character and virtues is an ancient Greek idea and not for Christians. They think that the effort to develop character smacks of salvation by works or that such efforts are doomed to failure because only God can change a person's character. We cannot take such a simplistic view. To do so confuses salvation (justification) with the Christian life (sanctification).

Becoming Responsible People

First, Christians profess that salvation is based solely upon the merit and work of Jesus Christ, not on our ability to be Christlike. Who of us could ever be saved if it depended upon our works? Surprisingly, however, we discover that becoming like Jesus is a goal of the Christian life (Mt 5:48; Lk 6:40; Jn 13:14; 1 Cor 11:1 and 15:49; 2 Cor 3:18; Phil 2:1-13; Eph 5:1-2; Col 3:12-17; 1 Pet 2:21; 1 Jn 2:6 and 3:1-3). Our virtuous lives are a response to God's grace, not a means of obtaining his favor. Salvation gives us the freedom to be the people God created us to be and to do those things that glorify him (Eph 2:8-9).

Secondly, there is a sense in which consciously practicing a virtue will eventually change our attitudes and feelings. For example, Eric could choose to view the irate physician as someone who is truly concerned about his patients rather than interpreting his anger as a personal insult. By doing so he could respond to him on a professional level rather than becoming angry and defensive. Looking for the best in people makes us feel better about those who would ordinarily annoy us. William Glasser's "Reality Therapy" is based on the premise that if we act in responsible ways, others will respect us, and we will respect ourselves. In the process we become responsible people.[10]

In chapter six we saw that Christian values flow from the character of God—from his personal nature, his goodness and his holiness. The Greeks had the right idea when they stressed that the way to become a morally excellent person was to follow the model of a philosopher-teacher: to observe him, interact with him and imitate him. Jesus chose this method to train the future leaders of the church, and they in turn continued teaching by his example (Mk 3:13-19; 2 Tim 2:2). The often maligned apprenticeship model of earlier nursing education relied heavily on teaching by modeling. Again, mentoring is being recognized by nurse educators as a powerful method for teaching values.[11]

If you want to develop Christian character, you need to be committed to God's concerns or values. To do this you must observe his character, interact with him and imitate him. Christians through the centuries have spoken of imitating Christ.

The influence of Jesus on his followers was so powerful that when their enemies observed their courage and readiness to suffer, "they took note that these men had been with Jesus" (Acts 4:13). "The communities, which they founded in the name of Jesus, became recognizably and distinctly different, because they worshiped him."[12] We absorb, almost unconsciously, the influence of great leaders, as did Christ's followers. But we are called on, as were Jesus' first disciples, to consciously imitate him. We follow in his steps. Jesus claims to be "the way" (Jn 14:6), and Christians are called "followers of the Way" (Acts 9:2; 16:17; 18:25; 19:9; 22:4; 24:14, 22).

Being Christian nurses, then, means that we follow Jesus, that we walk in his way and that we model our lives on his. Though we are separated from his early life by centuries and culture, the way he lived still provides an example for us in our work.

We, in turn, become models, influencing those who work with us and observe us in action. The power of such influence is not sufficiently recognized. How many young nurses have been encouraged to persist in their efforts to understand a difficult patient because a more experienced nurse modeled skill, caring and patience in a similar situation? Conversely, how often have idealistic young nurses been disillusioned by older colleagues who model attitudes and behavior that are disrespectful toward patients?

For example, Sandy, who was a new graduate, became extremely anxious about cleaning a tracheostomy for the first time. The patient, Mrs. Mathy, picked up Sandy's anxiety and became frightened. Each time Sandy approached with the suction catheter, Mrs. Mathy exhaled forcefully and blew out the entire tracheostomy tube. The third time, the white plastic tube became lost in the sheets, and the anxiety level of both the patient and the nurse peaked. Sandy remembered watching one of her older colleagues praying with patients when they were upset. She decided to try it. She put her hand on Mrs. Mathy's shoulder and quietly said, "I think we need to pray." As she prayed simply about the situation, both Sandy and Mrs. Mathy relaxed. Sandy quickly found the tube and gently replaced it. She continued the cleaning without difficulty.

Chris, another new graduate, had a very different experience. She began as a conscientious and compassionate nurse, taking time to listen to patients carefully. Gradually she noticed that most of the other nurses on her unit did not spend much time with patients unless they were giving physical care. They seemed to prefer talking to one another over listening to patients. During report some nurses would even turn off call lights without answering them, remarking, "That's just Mr. Rogers; he always has his light on." Before long Chris found herself thinking and acting like her coworkers.

Philosophers and theologians who write about character and virtue ethics argue that virtues are necessarily related to specific traditions. They are communicated through stories, the common narratives of those traditions. It is not really possible to speak generically about virtues because there is no universal understanding of how virtues should be recognized or defined. For example, justice is considered a universal value, but how justice is defined varies widely according to the tradition or community using the term. To some justice means equality; to others, justice is appropriate punishment for a crime. Justice to a "pro-choice" advocate means giving a woman control over her body. To a "pro-life" advocate justice is protecting the life of an unborn child.

Another example, beneficence (doing good), is also a "universal value," but what is good can only be defined in the context of a cultural and religious tradition. I might regard praying with patients as doing good, but someone from a different (or no) religious tradition might regard it as harmful. The "Baby Jane Doe" case of several years ago provides another example of differing perceptions of doing good. One side insisted that doing good was refusing to treat correctable life-threatening problems in a Down's syndrome newborn (to eliminate long-term pain and suffering for the baby and its family). The other side insisted that doing good required that surgery be performed so that the baby would live. Thus, the kinds of virtues (and related vices) and their meaning are found within a specific cultural and religious tradition. For the Christian nurse, that tradition is the Christian community as we find it described in the Bible, church history and our own churches and Christian fellowship groups.

Identifying with the Saints

Traditions are embodied in the lives of people. Each tradition has its "saints," those persons who have become models of virtue. Thus, if we want to know what the virtue of compassion looks like, we look to the saints as our models. A great example of compassion today is Mother Theresa. Her virtue is recognized by Christians and Hindus, as well as the secular press, as the embodiment of Christian compassion. She is teaching the world how to care by her example. For examples of justice, we can look to early leaders in American nursing such as Mary Eliza Mahoney (the first black professional nurse, who worked for acceptance of blacks in nursing) and Lillian Wald (pioneer in public health nursing and advocate for the urban poor).

As we identify with the "saints" and follow their example we become just and compassionate persons ourselves. We become like them. In turn we become models for others. (See Jn 13:15; 1 Thess 1:6-7; 1 Tim 4:12; 1 Pet 2:21 and 5:2-3.) *We* belong to a community of interdependent persons. As we accept our role in the ongoing drama of a people, our lives become our own. They become our own, not because we create them in the first place, but because we accept them as our own. In so doing we participate in the community of which we are a part with its traditions, values and saints.

Being in that Christian tradition bears directly on our work in nursing. Circumstances in nursing become a way to develop my character.

What happens at church, worship, fellowship, while learning and in personal devotions deepens our understanding of the Christian tradition. All of these shape who we are and how we view and experience our work.

Being a Christian Nurse
Today we hear that our religion is private and should be separate from our world of work. If this is the case for us, we are in danger of living a divided life. Being a Christian requires us to live by Christian values despite the values of the nursing community that surrounds us.

Christian nurses—all of us who acknowledge Jesus Christ as Lord and Savior—belong to the great tradition of men and women who believed in and obeyed God from the beginning (Heb 12:1). Nursing, as it has developed since the days of Christ, is part of that tradition. Christian nurses belong to a long line of women and men who imitated Christ in caring for the sick, becoming like him in attitudes and character. Being imitators of Christ does not mean, of course, that they (or we for that matter) achieved perfection. With all their flaws, we can find stories of compassion, courage and generosity among the saints for our edification.

A Historical Look
We in North America are not attuned to history. In nursing, especially, the focus is on moving ahead rather than looking back. We need to return to the history books. Dolan and Fitzpatrick's *Nursing and Society*,[13] for example, includes a wealth of stories of Christian saints. The tradition may glorify these men and women, and we can be prepared to sift fact from idealism, but the riches are still there. Pastor Everett Wilson, writing about the crisis in health care in the United States, urges readers to consider the history of the hospital movement in Western history. Medieval monasteries and cathedrals established

hostels for the indigent. Not until the nineteenth century did hospitals rent space to private patients. Today, hospitals have become places of convenience for the middle class, who see themselves as consumers. "Somehow," insists Wilson, "health care must move beyond asking, 'Who can pay?' to 'Who is my neighbor?' "[14]

Knowing the Christian influence in the history of health care and nursing helps us to put our own lives into that story. An appreciation for our heritage enhances our sense of having a role in a grand, on-going drama. We need not create our own meaning out of the struggles and frustrations in nursing. Instead, we find meaning in the story of God's redemption of his creation and our call to be participants with him in healing and re-creation. In this way we refocus on those virtues that characterize the redeeming God. We strive to make these virtues part of our character as well.

Present and Future Nursing Concerns

Nurses sometimes feel that it is difficult to be moral because the climate in which they work does not support morally excellent behavior. What they have in mind are things like short staffing, requests to work double shifts, or shortages of equipment and beds. In such settings nurses may be tempted to chart procedures that have not been completed, or they may "not see" patients who are incontinent, leaving them for the next shift. Although the temptation increases and some nurses may indeed succumb, such a view is both simplistic and fatalistic. It is fatalistic because this view sees nurses only as passive victims who are influenced by a bad environment. It is simplistic because it assumes that we can be moral only if we are supported by our immediate environment. It assumes that nurses have no power for change.

The health care crisis is only going to increase in the foreseeable future. Rising costs, budget deficits (including the federal deficit), and increasing numbers of chronically ill and frail elderly will push the system to its limits. While some nurses may indeed continue working in settings where equipment and resources are abundant, increasing numbers will be working with large numbers of seriously ill patients and a minimum of staff, supplies and equipment. How will Christian nurses respond to increasingly crowded nursing homes? to the closing of inner city hospitals that cared primarily for the poor? to private hospitals that refuse to care for patients without insurance? It won't be easy. We cannot be idealists alone.

Earlier I suggested that a renewed concern with character would contribute to the renewal of nursing. Deciding how to be moral in such stressful situations will require mature Christian character that has been shaped by the values of Jesus. It will require the support and counsel of fellow Christians who, with us, are actively seeking to walk in the living tradition of those who, with Jesus, work because our Father is working (Jn 5:17).

Virtuous nurses will struggle with suffering. Our culture, with its present values of progress and self-fulfillment, has no answer for suffering, no way to think about it. All that science and technology can do for suffering is to eliminate it and, more and more, that means eliminating the suffering person. Many overwhelmingly complex issues that confront us stem from our inability to deal with suffering and death. New Age thinking in health care is one attempt to deal with suffering, but it does so by trivializing it. Most religions provide a way to think about and bear suffering, but only Jesus Christ is the suffering God who stays with sufferers. Nurses who are like him in character will stay with those who suffer, drawing on his strength within his community.

Discussion Questions

Context for Discussion: Romans 5:1-5

   a. According to this passage, how does Christian character develop?

   b. In what ways have your difficult experiences ended up producing hope?

1. Often, when we pray for a virtue, such as love, God sends someone into our lives to test its limits. For example, Nancy prayed that she would be able to love Wanda, a coworker who was arrogant and sarcastic. Soon after that Wanda was promoted to head nurse. After her promotion Wanda became even more overbearing and critical. What positive steps could Nancy take in developing the virtue of love toward Wanda?

2. What one virtue would you most like to develop? For what reasons?

3. List and discuss some concrete steps you could take to develop this virtue.

8

STRATEGY FOR DISCIPLESHIP

Judith Allen Shelly

As I entered the mall, a young family caught my eye. The children, about ages five and seven, were pleading with their mother, "Please, Mom, don't make me hold your hand! I'll stay with you. I promise." She conceded, but before long the seven-year-old child had charged ahead to take the lead and the five-year-old one had darted off to look at an enticing toy display.

Too often our attempts at discipleship show a similar pattern. We make a well-intentioned, passionate commitment to the Lord, fully intending to do his will. But then his pace seems too slow, and the path seems clear so we try to run ahead of God. Or we may be faithfully following him when we happen to pass something that is our heart's desire—the perfect job, the ideal spouse, the chance to get out of a difficult situation—and our eyes are diverted. The diversion seems so attractive that it never occurs to us that the Lord may have other plans.

The frustrated mother in the shopping scene solved the problem by grabbing both children firmly by the hand saying, "Okay, you blew it, now you're sticking with me." God never does that.

Following Jesus

The essence of discipleship is following Jesus. It is something we choose to do. Jesus never forced anyone to follow him. In fact, he earnestly discouraged some would-be disciples (Mt 8:19-22; Mk 5:18-19). Discipleship is a learning process in which God allows us to fail, then dusts us off and trusts us to begin again. Even a cursory look at the behavior of the disciples in the Gospels, prods a reader to ask, "When are these guys going to catch on?" It seems they did the wrong thing more often than not, yet Jesus patiently stuck with them. Eventually most of them were in leadership positions in the early church.

There are no short-cuts to Christian maturity, and apart from the Bible, there is no guidebook. Discipleship is the process described in 2 Corinthians 3:18:

And we, who with unveiled faces all reflect the Lord's glory, are being transformed into his likeness with ever-increasing glory. . . .

While discipleship occurs in a community, it is different for each individual. I cannot impose my experience of discipleship on you, nor claim it to be normative for anyone else. For example, Peter, James and John all vividly witnessed the glory of God on the Mount of Transfiguration (Mk 9:2-8; Lk 9:28-36). Yet, they each had a different lesson to learn before growing to maturity in Christ (Mt 20:20-28; Mk 9:33-35; Lk 9:46). When Peter asked Jesus what was in store for John, Jesus essentially told him that it was none of his business (Jn 21:20-22).

Most of us would prefer to have a checklist of Christian values so we could periodically grade ourselves on our progress in discipleship. When I teach ethics workshops, someone invariably says in exasperation, "Just tell us the Christian position so we don't have to be so wishy-washy!" Discipleship is not being wishy-washy, although it is not simply adherence to a list of rules. It is walking so closely with Jesus that we can hear his voice guiding us in the decision-making process. He also will make us aware of issues on which we must take a stand. The prophet Isaiah proclaimed:

> Though the Lord may give you the bread of adversity and the water of affliction, yet your Teacher will not hide himself any more, but your eyes shall see your Teacher. And when you turn to the right or when you turn to the left, your ears shall hear a word behind you, saying, "This is the way; walk in it." (Is 30:20-21 NRSV)

Discipleship is constantly focusing our eyes and tuning our ears on the Teacher, seeking his will for every aspect of life. The lessons may become harder, or at least more complex, as you mature. Discipleship is never easy.

Risk Taking

For instance, Alicia grew up in a home where money was always tight. After graduating from nursing school and starting a job, seeing her savings mount up gave her a new sense of security. She had never had much money to give away before, so her giving continued to be minimal and erratic. After a while she began to feel convicted that she should tithe her income, including what was already in the bank. It was a tough struggle, but she finally did it. She was amazed at how good she felt. She really did not miss the money. She gradually increased the amount of money she gave away, enjoying the feeling of participation in so many ministries. Then she began to invest her time in a ministry that she supported at an inner-city clinic. Her primary job there was doing health assessments and well-baby checkups on Saturday mornings. Part of the assessment guide she used asked about spiritual matters. Discussions about faith seemed to follow naturally. She was thrilled to see several of her regular clients eventually become Christians. After about a year of volunteering, the clinic director asked to see her.

"Alicia, you seem to have a real gift for working with our clients. Not only do you have strong assessment skills, but you have a deep compassion for the people, which clearly communicates God's love to them. Would you be willing to consider working with us full-time? Our funding is very low, so we could not offer you much of a salary, and you also would need to help raise your support by asking friends and local churches to contribute to the clinic."

Alicia struggled. She had a strong commitment to the clinic and had been thinking about how she would like to work there full-time. She had even wondered if God might be calling her to do that. Now the sense of calling was reinforced by the director's request, but to take a substantial cut in salary and to ask people for money was repugnant to her. Her stomach tied itself in knots.

What Alicia did with the knots was discipleship. She wrestled with whether financial security was an idol to her and whether she was willing to follow Jesus even if it seemed irrational. She talked with her pastor and asked her Bible study group to pray with her. She began to spend large periods of time reading Scripture and praying. After a month of agonizing, Alicia decided to take the job.

The direction in which the Lord leads you may be different from the way he leads your friends. Barbara struggled with a situation similar to Alicia's, but she concluded that God was calling her to her present job and the extra financial support it enabled her to give to the ministry.

Jesus calls us to discipleship so that we may learn from him and teach others (Mt 4:19 and 28:19; 2 Tim 2:2). We are not learning simply to heighten our own spirituality. Discipleship must be contagious. It prepares us to tell other people about Jesus so that they also can become his disciples. In our culture our lives often speak louder than words, but words must accompany our actions or we are merely witnessing to ourselves (1 Pet 3:15). A Christian who does not overflow with spontaneous evangelism may be seriously lacking in true discipleship.

Total Commitment

Discipleship affects how we do our secular jobs, the way we relate to other people, our understandings (and acts) of justice and compassion, as well as the "spiritual" things we do. Prayer, Bible study and Christian community are the equipment God provides for being disciples. They are not the ends, but the means, for discipleship. Too often we measure our spiritual health by our "Christian activities." If I have my Quiet Time regularly, attend a weekly Bible study (maybe even lead it), and participate in worship and church activities, I'm okay. After all, I don't have time for much more. But discipleship is more.

Consider a man who graduates from nursing school, passes the State Board Examinations, reads nursing journals daily, joins the state nurses association and attends district meetings faithfully, but never practices nursing. He is technically a nurse, he has a license to prove it, but he is not nursing. In the same way, we can go through all the motions of Christian activities. Until we follow Jesus in every aspect of our lives, though, we are not practicing discipleship. The spiritual disciplines are essential, just as nursing education is essential for the nurse, but they must lead to changes in character and lifestyle. If we are truly following Jesus, living in a dynamic relationship with him, our lives will begin to reflect his character.

While discipleship is not easy, the alternative is worse. Faith without discipleship eventually withers. When we run ahead of God, we fool ourselves into thinking that we are in control. After a while we begin to think we don't need God. Only a dramatic failure pulls us back to reality. If we become distracted by the enticements of the world around us, it is easy to grow comfortable and lose sight of the kingdom of God. There is nothing wrong with enjoying the good gifts God provides, but they can become a snare that prevents us from moving out of our "comfort zones" to work for justice and mercy in the world. Anything that pulls us away from total dependence upon God weakens our faith.

Lifelines in a Hectic Life

If discipleship is following Jesus, then Bible study and prayer are the communication that keeps the relationship alive and growing. The Bible is God's love letter and instruction manual for us. We never outgrow our need to continually study the Bible. Even old familiar passages take on new meaning as our life experiences change. The Holy Spirit works through the Scriptures to give us the Lord's perspective on the world around us. God speaks to us through the Bible.

Prayer is equally important. Prayer is not a way of manipulating God; nor is it a one-way telegram from us to him. It is the intimate conversation between God and those he loves. Think of the communication you have with someone you love. There are times when you express your needs, ask for help and talk about the needs of others; but there is much more. You tell that person what you appreciate and admire in him, and you thank him for what he does for you. You discuss your goals and dreams. You bat ideas around, and sometimes you merely sit in expressive silence. You can communicate across a room with your eyes and body language. You celebrate together when things go well, and you cry together when they don't. You eventually begin to think and act like the person you love. That is how prayer influences our discipleship and shapes Christian character.

Many of us have grown up with a legalistic view of personal devotions. We have been told that Jesus ". . . in the morning, while it was still dark, . . . got up and went off to a solitary place, where he prayed"

(Mk 1:35). Therefore, some of us believe that we must get up at 4:30 A.M. and have our Quiet Time before work.

I am not a morning person. I can't carry on a pleasant conversation with anyone before 7:00 A.M., much less with God. For years I felt guilty about my substandard spirituality. Then I discovered that the Bible doesn't say that Jesus always prayed before dawn. Sometimes he left the crowds in the middle of the day to go off by himself and pray (Mt 8:18; Mk 6:46). Other times he prayed in the evening, after his work was done (Mt 14:23). Sometimes he prayed all night (Lk 6:12). And perhaps his most famous prayer (Jn 17) was in a garden after supper (Mt 26:36). He also prayed from the cross, in the midst of his suffering, interceding for others (Lk 23:33).

The time of day that we set for Bible reading and prayer is probably not important. It is important, though, to discipline ourselves to spend regular time with God. While even that may sound legalistic, our human nature requires it. If we don't get into the habit of setting a time for daily devotions, another habit will take its place. That happens in our human relationships as well. If I don't sit with my children when they get home from school to talk about their day and go over their school papers, it doesn't get done. If my husband and I don't set aside time before bed to talk and pray together, we get lost in the daily routine and never really communicate anything other than logistical information. We need a daily time to talk with God. It should be the same time each day, if possible, so that it becomes a habit.

Daily devotions are when we can talk with God about everyday thoughts and concerns. The Scriptures encourage, challenge and direct us. Praising God puts life into perspective, reminding us that he is in control and cares. Confessing sin assures us of God's forgiveness. Thanking God, besides being polite, reminds us that all good things come from him. Interceding for others makes us partners with God and his people in the work of his kingdom (Rom 15:30-32; Eph 6:18-

20). Examine the prayers of Jesus (Mt 6:9-15; Lk 23:34, 46; Jn 17) and Paul (Eph 1; Phil 1:3-11; Col 1:9-20; 1 Thess 1:2-3; 1 Tim 1:12-17) and the hymns of praise in Revelation (11:17-18; 15:3-4; 19:6-6) for examples of how to pray. The Psalms also provide rich examples of prayer.

Practical helps for intercessory prayer include making a list of prayer concerns. If it becomes too long, divide it over several days. Whenever you assure people that you'll pray for them, be sure to jot a note to yourself. Missionary prayer letters and prayer calendars with requests for each day can help you pray more specifically for others. Many people find that keeping a journal and writing down prayers each day can be helpful and encouraging. You can review your journal months and years later and remember how God has worked.

"I know prayer and Bible study are important, but I just don't have time every day," you may say. Most people don't.

There are two things to keep in mind. First, prayer is work. It is part of our assigned job description as a Christian. It is a top priority. Secondly, prayer and Bible study often save time and work. While most of us feel guilty for not spending more time with God, we also may feel guilty when we do take time to just pray and read the Bible. Stopping to spend extended time in prayer seems like goofing off when we could be *doing something*. North Americans are "doers." We value action. Even when activity is futile, we continue to spin our wheels to feel better. In those times of wheel spinning we need to pull back and, like Jesus, leave the crowds to pray.

One of the most helpful disciplines that I have found is to spend a full day in prayer once a month. A whole day sounds like a long time, but it goes quickly. I follow the same pattern of praise, confession, thanksgiving and intercession as in my daily devotions, but in a much more relaxed manner. I sit with my Bible open and read psalms of praise, confession and thanksgiving. I sing hymns. I may take a walk and thank God for what I see, or merely look around me and thank him for the gifts he has given. Then I pull out all the missionary prayer letters and various prayer requests that have collected since the last day of prayer and intercede for people. Finally, I talk to the Lord about my thoughts, concerns and dreams, asking for his advice and direction. I have been amazed over the years to see how God answers prayer so clearly. Plans fall into place that one day earlier seemed impossible. Solutions to long-standing problems suddenly appear evident. New ideas take shape. I don't think God is speaking to me any more clearly after a day of prayer than he was earlier, but my ears are usually much more tuned to listen to him.

Between the special times set apart for prayer, we are to "pray continually" (1 Thess 5:17) "on all occasions" (Eph 6:18). The discipline of maintaining a constant conversation with God can radically change your life. For instance, let's say you are working on a surgical unit. Mrs. Johnson, who will be discharged tomorrow, has pushed her call light for the fourth time in the past half hour. As you go to answer the light there is time for a quick prayer. It may be a prayer of confession, "Lord, forgive me for being angry." You also can pray for wisdom. "Help me to know what Mrs. Johnson *really* needs this time." When you get to Mrs. Johnson's room, you'll have a completely different attitude toward her. You may begin to hear her unspoken concerns in a new way.

Many situations which annoy and frustrate us, like waiting in grocery lines or sitting in traffic, also can be opportunities to pray. People who pray constantly live in hopeful expectation, knowing that God is actively involved in every situation, despite how bleak it may appear.

Praying constantly is a mindset. It is to work consciously as a partner with God. It is not a substitute for times of undistracted, quiet meditation, but it is essential for true discipleship.

The Strength of Group Prayer

Jesus also instructed us to pray with others (Mt 18:19-20). Have you ever noticed how discussing a situation with a group of people can expand your understanding of the subject under consideration? Praying together can do even more. For instance, Leslie worked in a community health agency that was considering a strike. As Leslie prayed, all she could think about was, "Lord, please don't let them vote for the strike!" Then she began to pray with several of her colleagues, as well as the agency supervisor. They prayed about all the issues involved, including the adversarial relationships that were developing between management and staff, and between staff who were for and those who were against the strike. In the end the strike took place, but working relationships were healed rather than severed because they had been praying together.

Group prayer is powerful. It is part of the disciple's ministry to others. Consider the scene in Acts 4. Peter and John had just been arrested, tried, warned not to preach anymore, then released. The first thing they did was to go to their friends to report what had happened. You would think that the friends would have been fearful, maybe telling Peter and John to tone their message down a bit to avoid future confrontations with the law. Instead, they began to pray:

> After they prayed, the place where they were meeting was shaken.
> And they were all filled with the Holy Spirit and spoke the word
> of God boldly. (Acts 4:31)

A similar scene occurred in a local hospital. As Marilyn cared for Mrs. Ruiz, she became aware of her deep spiritual needs. When Marilyn offered to pray for her, Mrs. Ruiz gratefully agreed. After discharge Mrs. Ruiz wrote to the hospital administrator, praising Marilyn's nursing care, including the prayer. The administrator immediately called Marilyn into his office and reprimanded her for praying with a patient. That evening Marilyn told her Nurses Christian Fellowship group about what happened. The group began to pray for Marilyn and for the hospital administration to be open to spiritual care. The nurses in the group who worked in that hospital began openly to meet spiritual needs and chart their interventions. Within a year the hospital sponsored an in-service education seminar on spiritual care and encouraged nurses to attend the seminar so that they could begin meeting patients' spiritual needs.

As Christians, we are members of the body of Christ (1 Cor 12:12). We cannot operate solo. It is the whole body, which is the expression of Christ in the world today, not each individual part. We are incomplete without the rest of the body; therefore, we need to be active participants in a local church and in the Christian community in our work and living settings. Every disciple needs to worship regularly with a congregation. We need to pray with other Christians who are our colleagues and with those in our home. It takes effort to set group Bible study, worship and prayer as top priority, especially with the complications of scheduling, but fellowship with other Christians is not an optional activity for disciples. It is a central part of our job description.

Measuring Output

Just as a balanced fluid intake and output are essential for our physical bodies, spiritual intake and output also must be kept in dynamic equilibrium. If setting aside time to spend with the Lord is more difficult than a simple juggling of priorities, then it may be time to start keeping track of your spiritual intake and output. The values of our culture encourage us to drive ourselves to spiritual dehydration. Most nurses enter the profession with high ideals. They want to lovingly and compassionately care for people. The reality of the workplace, with emphasis on efficiency, cost-effectiveness and productivity, often clouds the human and spiritual dimensions of nursing. Look at your findings in chapter three. If you found a large discrepancy between your personal values and the values that govern your nursing practice in your work setting, then you may be headed toward dehydration. The next chapter will provide some practical help for changing your work environment. The family is another area of spiritual intake and output. Ideally, our families should be a source of intake, but for many they require more output. Lack of quality time may lead to friction and guilt. Spouses who do not share spiritual concerns, children who are rebelling and parents who are unsupportive can be devastating. Many Christians live with the scars, or the continuing tragedy, of physical and emotional abuse. Even families who share a faith commitment may struggle with interpersonal conflict, financial loss, illness and death.

If you find that your family requires more output than you have to give, it is time to make some changes. For simple problems, the solution may merely be to schedule more time for the family. That could require cutting back on the hours you work in nursing or the time spent in volunteer work. A trusted friend or pastor can help you think of some creative alternatives. For more complicated problems, it may be necessary to find professional counseling. Counseling can be a significant source of intake. It requires that we admit our neediness and our desire for help.

You may even need to assess your church intake and output. Jesus established the church to restore and equip us to serve him. It, too, should be a source of intake, but instead can become a drain on the disciple's resources. Some Christians get in the output mode in their churches and never take advantage of the intake available to them. For instance, Rosemary taught Sunday school, sang in the choir, served on three committees, and was treasurer of the women's organization. She also worked full-time. But whenever there was a church function in which she was not directly serving, she did not attend. When I asked her about that she replied, "I wouldn't feel comfortable coming if I didn't have a job to do." She has since begun to balance her intake and output activities in the church, learning to feel comfortable and even enjoy the intake.

Being involved in the community in which you live is part of the responsibility of discipleship. We can't share the Good News with our neighbors if we don't even know them. Community involvement can be fun. The relationships formed and tasks accomplished may contribute to your spiritual intake. Delivering "Meals on Wheels" can be deeply rewarding. Talking with the hurting mother of one of your children's classmates and helping her find faith and hope in Jesus can be exhilarating. Running for political office may enable you to make positive changes in your community. Yet, the community also can absorb all that you will give. While it is important for disciples to serve the community, you can easily give until you have no more time or energy. Community service needs to be balanced with other demands for output and with the intake necessary to make it effective.

Planning for Intake

We write care plans for our patients, but seldom think about intentionally planning for spiritual intake beyond the very basic activities. Take time to think about your needs for spiritual intake.

☐ How much time do you spend really studying the Bible? Do you need to set a plan for personal Bible study? Are you currently in a small group Bible study? What kind of study would meet your needs right now?

☐ How many Christian books have you read lately? Which ones would you like to read? When? Do you read the *Journal of Christian Nursing?* What are you reading to help you understand current trends in our society? in nursing?

☐ Can you pray with your family/housemates? Do you need to make changes in family priorities? Do you need to seek professional help?

☐ Are you committed to a local church? Do you worship regularly? Are you taking advantage of opportunities for learning and spiritual growth? Do you know people at church well enough to feel like you are a part of a Christian community/family?

☐ What mature Christian could be a mentor for you? Do you have a trusted friend who could help you assess your needs for intake and output? Do you have a prayer partner?

☐ How can you learn from other Christian nurses? Is there a Nurses' Christian Fellowship in your area? If not, could you start one? Can you attend a workshop or conference to help you integrate Christian faith and nursing?

☐ Are you involved in your community too much? not enough?

☐ Are you intentionally planning time for refreshment? Do you schedule opportunities for spiritual growth on days off and vacations, or do these times just pass in a fog? Have you considered a "sabbatical" (like a summer of camp nursing or six months in an inner city clinic)?

☐ Is it time for a major change? Would returning to school refresh your vision? Have you dreamed of doing a different kind of nursing? Have you considered going overseas?

Planning for Balanced Discipleship

Balanced discipleship requires us to choose our values according to what is most important to God. It is seeking first the kingdom of God and his righteousness (Mt 6:33) rather than getting caught up into the materialism, narcissism and radical autonomy that drives our culture. Jesus gives us the good news of freedom from self.

Priorities set by disciples of Jesus Christ will probably look strange to the world around us. They also might jar people into listening to our message. Recently, a respected physician resigned from the staff of a local hospital because of its policy on abortion. His willingness to sacrifice significant income caused people to listen to his reasons. Former president Jimmy Carter is gaining new respect today, not for high profile appearances, but because people have seen him in work-clothes, hammering nails into houses for the poor. When Christians are willing to sacrifice financial security, prestige and power to live out the demands of the gospel, the world begins to take notice.

Our culture tells us that we must conform to be credible. Christians have believed that lie for too long. Conformity with the world merely allows us to blend in with the crowd and become invisible. Discipleship requires us to follow Jesus in ways that boldly confront the validity of accepted cultural values. In doing so we need the strength and support of the Christian community, because confrontation may lead to rejection and persecution. In some areas of Central and South America Bible studies are viewed as subversive by the government, because Christians who have gained a biblical understanding of justice are beginning to confront the status quo. In Namibia and South Africa Black pastors are arrested and often jailed for merely conducting pastoral functions because Black churches have been the gathering point for opposition to apartheid. Discipleship is a commitment to follow Jesus Christ, despite the consequences. Jesus called discipleship a "narrow gate" which leads to a difficult road, but the road ends in life (Mt 7:13-14)—overflowing life (Jn 10:10).

Discussion Questions
Context for Discussion: Luke 10:25-37
   a. What principles of discipleship are given in this passage?
   b. How is loving God related to loving our neighbor?

   1. What is the most difficult aspect of discipleship for you?
   2. As you read through the spiritual intake assessment on pages 113-14, which areas need attention in your life? Discuss ideas for developing a plan to increase your intake.
   3. What special gifts (abilities, talents, skills) has God given you? List them and share with the group. If the group knows each other well enough, you could also ask group members to write down the gifts they see in one another.
   4. How do the unique gifts God has given you fit together with the gifts of other Christian nurses to enable you to influence nursing for Jesus Christ?
   5. What can you do if you feel you are fighting battles all alone?

9
A STRATEGY
FOR INFLUENCE

Arlene B. Miller & Judith Allen Shelly

Kelly liked working at St. Luke's Medical Center. Formerly a church-related hospital, it had recently been acquired by a for-profit corporation. The corporation seemed to hold nurses in high esteem. Working conditions and benefits had markedly improved with the new management. The new owners also seemed to have a deep commitment to meeting the total needs of people, including their spiritual needs. Then one evening Kelly was assigned to the emergency department, and she began to question the ethics of her employer.

First, a woman in hard labor was admitted, then suddenly transferred to another hospital because she did not have health insurance. She was fully dilated and her blood pressure was 188/102. Kelly was appalled. Next, an automobile accident occurred within one block of the hospital, but the critically injured victims were sent to City Hospital ten miles away. No one knew if they had insurance, but it was assumed that they did not because they were Black. Kelly wondered if such a decision was even legal. Then, a prominent businessman came in complaining of mild chest pains. He was immediately given priority and quickly admitted to the Coronary Care Unit. His discomfort turned out to be indigestion. By the end of her shift, Kelly felt angry and disgusted.

Kelly is not the only nurse who has been frustrated by the injustice of the health-care system. Basic to our understanding of justice is an underlying assumption that there are certain universal human rights that must be respected. Something deep within us cries out, "It's just not fair!" On the other hand, most Christians feel uncomfortable discussing rights. We would rather talk about responsibilities and let the secular world battle over their rights. The problem leaves us in a quandary. Therein lies our sense of powerlessness and fear of facing the injustice that surrounds us.

Is the struggle for human rights a proper concern for Christians? Let's turn to the Scriptures for guidance. Proverbs 31 lists the important teachings that King Lemuel learned from his mother. Verse 9 states, "Speak up and judge fairly; defend the rights of the poor and needy." The prophet Jeremiah blasts the leaders of Judah saying, "They do not defend the rights of the poor" (Jer 5:28b). Ethicist Stephen Charles Mott proposes a "biblical list of human rights" as being:

> the sanctity of life; the right not to be permanently deprived of land; equality in the means of livelihood and, where this is not possible, equality of opportunity; the right to rest from work one day in seven; the right of a servant of God not to be a servant of anyone else; the right to be protected from the arbitrary exercise of power; equality

before the law or equal subjection to the law of all classes.[1]
When we look at the Ten Commandments as foundational to the biblical understanding of justice, most of these rights are implied. If we view the commandments as positive principles for justice, the rights become even clearer. "You shall not kill" assumes a right to life; however, taken further it also implies the right to access to the requirements for life: food, water, shelter, safety and health. Access to basic health care is essential for life. Refusing to care for an eclamptic woman in labor or critically injured accident victims violates their right to life.

"You shall not steal" leads us beyond a basic understanding of not taking hospital supplies home with us. It assumes a person's right to property. It means being concerned about the resources of AIDS patients that are being depleted by mounting health-care costs. "You shall not bear false witness" assumes a right to truth. It requires us to provide accurate information to the public about health care, nutrition and healthful lifestyle and to obtain truly informed consent before medical procedures. "You shall not commit adultery" stems from the right to faithfulness and respect for confidentiality in all relationships. "You shall not covet" is based on a person's right to be treated fairly. It means refusing to seek personal gain at the expense of others.

When the lawyer approached Jesus in Luke 10:25-37, saying that he had kept the commandments, Jesus replied by telling the story of the Good Samaritan and saying, "Go and do likewise." Too often we are like that lawyer. We are satisfied to think we can please God by keeping a moral code as a checklist for personal righteousness. But he expects us to go beyond the letter of the law to care for our needy neighbors and to defend their rights.

Mott asserts, "Rights, properly defined, are as much a matter of responsibility as they are of freedom. Every right implies a duty" (p. 53). Whenever we claim an individual right, we must then insure that our neighbor is also given the same right. Therein lies the responsibility.

Learning from One Another

Kelly was probably able to see the injustice in the Emergency Department more clearly than the regular personnel because she was pulled from her usual unit. We get numb to our own forms of injustice. At an international nursing conference a British nurse commented, "How can you, as a Christian, work in such an unfair system? In England everyone gets free health care." A Canadian public health nurse told how she visits every new mother in her territory. That is part of the government-provided health care. In the process she has discovered many correctable problems that would not have surfaced in the United States until after a child started school. In inner-city Philadelphia another friend gave me a tour of her neighborhood and the local clinic. "Most of these people don't seek health care until they are seriously ill. They can't afford it, or they don't speak enough English to communicate, or they are on drugs, or they just don't have enough basic health information to make wise choices," she told me.

We constantly hear about the superiority of health care in the United States, and although we may get frustrated with the specifics of the system, most of us believe that it is the best. Sometimes we must step out of our familiar settings to see the injustice that surrounds us. Even the step from being a provider to becoming a consumer of health care can open our eyes to injustice. Nursing is beginning to recognize the need for change,[2] but how hard are we willing to fight for it?

Barriers to basic health care abound for many people in our society. Age, sex, race, ethnic, social, diagnostic, geographical, educational and economic factors can prevent a person from obtaining adequate health care. Consider the following situations:

☐ "Randy" is a thirteen-month-old boy. He weighs eleven pounds, cannot sit, stand or crawl. He has not had any immunizations or well-baby checkups since leaving the hospital at birth. His mother is mildly retarded and thinks he is doing fine. She feeds him sixteen ounces of over-diluted formula and one scrambled egg a day.

□ "Donna" is a thirty-two-year-old mother of four who has been admitted to the hospital six times in the past year for various injuries. Each time she had an explanation for the cuts, burns and bruises. She never said that her husband was beating her. No one bothered to ask. Each time she was quickly discharged without any follow-up.

□ "Takako" recently moved to the United States from Japan. Soon after arriving she was admitted to a hospital with right upper quadrant pain. She was considered an ideal patient by the nurses. She never complained about anything. For two days after her cholecystectomy she received no pain medication. Although she experienced excruciating pain, she did not complain because it was culturally unacceptable. No one bothered to ask if she needed an analgesic.

□ "Barry" is a homeless alcoholic who is frequently admitted to a teaching hospital. He is often subjected to unnecessary, painful tests and procedures because the medical students view him as good clinical experience. Each time he is discharged he goes back out on the street with no continuing health care.

□ "David" recently tested positive for HIV. When his employer found out, David immediately lost his job and his health insurance. He finally found another job, but no insurance carrier would accept him because of his HIV-positive status.

□ "Jennie" is five months pregnant, but there is no medical care available within 100 miles of her rural home. She has not received any prenatal care.

□ "Atugonza" lives in rural Kenya. She has lost three children to diarrhea. A simple saline-and-sugar solution given orally would have saved their lives, but she did not know about it. Now her youngest child has diarrhea. He probably will die too.

□ "Linda" is a thirty-two-year-old single mother of four. She has metastatic cervical carcinoma. It could have been caught in an early stage with a routine pap test, but she had not had one for five years. Her health insurance did not cover any routine checkups, and money had been scarce since her divorce, so she felt that she could not afford health care except in emergencies.

Injustice surrounds us. When it is close to home we may be blind to it or we may excuse it by blaming the victim. It is easy to think that Linda had her priorities mixed up. Why didn't she see the importance of regular, preventive health care? We need to listen to her concerns before blaming her. Her choices may have been between food for her children and a pap test for herself.

To locate issues of injustice in health care we need to look around us and be willing to question the status quo. Which call lights on your unit go unanswered for long periods of time? How well are medical procedures explained before obtaining informed consent? Who are the people in your community who may be "falling through the cracks" of the health-care system? How are state and federal funds spent? How is our overconsumption affecting people in poorer countries?

Identifying Sources of Injustice in Health Care

Injustice begins at a very human and personal level. We live in a "fallen world." We are all sinful human beings who are shaped by our cultural values, suffer from ineptitude, selfishness and greed, often lack creativity and hope and fear disturbing the status quo. When we do recognize injustice around us, we often feel overwhelmed and powerless. We ask, "What can I do about it?" not as a way of finding out, but as an excuse for inaction.

What can we do? Plenty. But it may mean giving up some treasured cultural values. We live in a society that expects instant gratification, seeks convenience and comfort, and views newness as progress. It will take time—time you may think you don't have—to read, research and communicate. It probably will force you to change your lifestyle. Probably the most painful effect of identifying injustice is that it will put you at odds with those who are benefitting from the unjust practices. Those beneficiaries may include taxpayers, government officials, consumers, business leaders and, probably, your family. For some nurses, past and present, the consequences of seeking justice have been serious. Sonia is one of those nurses.

Sonia Umanzor was a senior nursing student in El Salvador when she was expelled from school for caring for war refugees whom the government was denying medical care. Eventually, she was hunted down by death squads. Many of her friends, her father and her fiancé were killed, but she eventually escaped to the United States. When confronted by her school's principal, she protested:

> In school we are told that a nurse's duty is to tend those who need help. To be a dedicated nurse I must use what I am learning to help those whose rights have been taken away.[3]

Sonia continues to use her skills in caring for refugees in the United States, many of whom are illegal immigrants.

When sinful individuals form corporations and governments the result is structural evil. Many multinational corporations, including U.S. companies, exploit poor countries to provide luxury items at low cost for richer countries.[4] In parts of Bolivia and Peru most farmers, including Christians, have been forced to raise coca plants (the raw material for cocaine) to survive. They are unable to make a living wage growing food because prices in the world market are so low.[5]

Governments also create and perpetuate injustice. Totalitarian governments tend to exploit the people to enrich the leaders. Democratic governments are swayed by the leaders' need for popular support to win re-election. Justice is seldom popular because it usually requires sacrifice on the part of the "haves" to care for the "have nots." Militarism also causes rampant injustice. If only a small fraction—some say five per cent—of the world's military budgets were spent on health care, the World Health Organization's goal, "Health for all by 2000," could easily be met.

When injustice is so much a part of our personal lives and societal systems, how can we even begin to recognize the problems? First, we must use that important nursing skill—*observation*. Consider the case situations listed above. "Randy," the thirteen-month-old failure-to-thrive baby, may be in your church nursery every Sunday morning. The nursery attendants are probably worried, but afraid to say anything for fear of offending someone. You have probably cared for "Donna," the abused wife, often. Approximately twenty-five per cent of women admitted to hospital emergency rooms are there because of injuries resulting from domestic violence.[6] "Takako," the silently suffering Japanese woman, could have been from any ethnic group whose customs are unfamiliar. How are people from other cultures treated by your health-care agency? Are they stereotyped? ignored? ridiculed? "Barry," the homeless alcoholic, appears in almost every teaching hospital as "fair game." Who is defending his rights?

Like each of the other case studies, "David" is not an isolated case. There are thousands of HIV-positive "Davids" in the United States today. What is being done to insure that they receive adequate health care as the disease progresses? As your awareness is heightened by one difficult situation, you become sensitized to the needs of others in similar circumstances.

"Linda," the young single mother dying of cervical cancer, may be your next-door neighbor or the patient you cared for last week. Just observing the facts might only serve to make you angry. Then you may begin to ask, "Why did something so preventable have to happen?" At that point you can begin to search for answers, and to find them you must *listen* to what Linda has to say.

"Jennie," the isolated pregnant woman, and "Atugonza," the Kenyan mother whose children died of diarrhea, live too far away for you to know them personally, but you have probably seen them on television or read about them in newspapers and magazines. You may have even heard about them from a visiting missionary. In an age of instant communication the problems of the remotest village in Africa appear daily in our living rooms. We are so barraged with information that we become numb. To adequately identify injustice in the world, though, we must *seek accurate information* from trusted sources. Christian publications, videos and first-person accounts from missionaries and church leaders can provide both facts and a Christian evaluation of the problem.

Finding Power to Help

The Christmas issue of our denominational world mission magazine arrived with a picture on the cover of a starving woman holding an empty bowl. It sat around unopened and unread for several weeks. Inside was a message of hope and empowerment, but the cover portrayed such an overwhelming problem that it took weeks to muster the strength to get beyond it.

The feeling of hopelessness at the tremendous injustice that surrounds us is probably what prevents us from seeing it at all. Most people beyond adolescence have clearly realized that they can't single-handedly change the world. With that loss of idealism usually comes a sense of powerlessness to change anything in society. Yet, God has endowed us with power and expects us to use it (Is 40:29; Acts 1:8). First, he has given us all *general power,* which includes moral influence and spiritual authority. Second, he has given each of us *situational power,* which comes from our education, experience, position or personal prestige.

You are the light of the world. A city built on a hill cannot be hid. No one after lighting a lamp puts it under the bushel basket, but on the lampstand, and it gives light to all in the house. In the same way, let your light shine before others, so that they may see your good works and give glory to your Father in heaven. (Mt 5:14-16 NRSV)

The power to do what is right can be a tremendous *moral influence*, but it is not easy. When "everyone else" is caught up in a pattern of injustice and indifference, simply acting justly shines as a bright light that gives courage to others. Lorna found herself in such a situation.

Lorna returned to nursing after being home with her children for seven years. She was quickly oriented to a surgical floor. Then the director of nursing told her, "The head nurse on this floor will be on medical leave for three months. You have more experience than any of the other RNs on 7 West, so I need you to be acting head nurse." Lorna discovered that she had walked into a complicated web of anger, distrust and deception. The entire staff seemed to hate each other. They told her that the head nurse had a "nervous breakdown" from working there. Lorna spent time talking with each staff member, trying to sort out their tales of discrimination and distrust of one another. She began working closely with them and helping them with unpleasant tasks. She modeled skilled and compassionate nursing care. She was also firm in setting limits and exposing incompetence. One alcoholic nurse, who abused several patients, was fired with the condition that she could be rehired after successfully completing a treatment program. Soon the staff began to trust and respect Lorna. They began to follow her example in relating to patients and to one another. Lorna became known for fair treatment. Eventually, they began to trust one another and enjoy working together.

Spiritual authority goes beyond moral influence. When Jesus called his disciples he "gave them authority to drive out evil spirits and to heal every disease and every sickness" (Mt 10:1). He further instructed them:

> But when they arrest you, do not worry about what to say or how to say it. At that time you will be given what to say, for it will not be you speaking, but the Spirit of your Father speaking through you. (Mt 10:19-20)

As Christians, and as nurses, we have been given the authority to speak out against evil and to heal. We go out with the promise that the Spirit will speak through us. That does not mean we can lift our hands to end all evil and cure every disease. Even Jesus did not do that. Instead, we have been given a job description with responsibility and commensurate authority to do the job. When Lorna suddenly found herself in charge of a difficult situation, she began to pray and asked others to pray with her. She also prayed openly with patients, and recorded it in the care plans and nurses' notes. She soon saw changes that could only have come from the Spirit working in their midst. From a human perspective, the situation seemed hopeless, but another power was at work.

Walking into a spiritual battlefield is serious business. Not only do we see the power of God, but the power of Satan becomes evident. Whenever Jesus cast out demons in the Bible, they confronted him with belligerence, name-calling, bargaining and attempts to stir up chaos. Lorna experienced tremendous upheaval in the process of change. Whenever you expose evil and injustice you can expect opposition. That is no excuse for avoiding confrontation. We have been given spiritual power, and we must not be afraid to use it. Besides moral influence and spiritual authority, God has given each of us some kind of *situational power*. Your *nursing education and experience* is one source of power. You may object. We have heard much about the powerlessness of nurses within the health-care system, but we do have power. First, we have power in terms of influence with the public. Most people trust nurses to be honest and caring. They also respect our knowledge of health care. Nurses are also approachable. How often are you asked for advice by people in your church and community? That is power.

We also have the potential for influence in our health-care agencies, nursing organizations and political structures. Part of our "powerlessness" stems from a fear of speaking out. Once you are willing to step out and become involved, you will find yourself being called upon for leadership roles. For example, Betsy became involved in her specialty nursing organization. She was distressed by its stand on abortion and sought to get at least equal representation of the pro-life position. Before long she was elected president of the regional division of the organization, not because everyone agreed with her, but because they respected her willingness to take a stand and stick by it.

Advanced education and position provide further influence within the nursing profession and the health-care system. Christians can continue to have a major influence in the shape and direction of nursing in the future by getting the degrees necessary to seek positions of leadership—and then being unafraid to speak out with moral influence and spiritual authority. Although many key leadership positions in nursing in the United States and worldwide are held by Christians, many of these nurses have been conditioned by the educational process to keep their spiritual convictions to themselves. We need to take our example from International Council of Nurses President Mo-Im Kim, who stated in her first press conference, "I myself am a Christian nurse."[7] Being a Christian nurse publicly enables you to influence nursing for Jesus Christ and bring Christian values back into the nursing profession.

Doing What Is Just

Stories of other nurses' influence may be inspiring, but we can always view those situations as exceptions. Most Christian nurses continue to feel frustrated and powerless in their work situations and haven't even begun to think of a wider influence. What can the average Christian nurse do to work for justice?

The first step is in *being a just person.* When King Solomon asked God for "a discerning heart to govern your people and to distinguish between right and wrong," God was pleased and granted his request (1 Kings 3:9). James tells us, "If any of you lacks wisdom, he should ask God, who gives generously to all without finding fault, and it will be given him" (Jas 1:5). Rather than feeling guilty about your lack of involvement in doing justice, you can begin to ask God to make you aware of injustice within your area of influence. Then you can begin to get involved right where you are.

Working for justice can become a guise for self-righteousness, so the just person must be careful to live under the lordship of Christ, seeking his will and direction. When Jesus was attacked for pursuing justice, he told his accusers, "My Father is always at his work to this very day, and I, too, am working" (Jn 5:17). Jesus knew that what he was fighting for was part of his Father's program.

We need to be equally sure that we are doing God's work and not just defending our own ideas. We must be willing to admit when we are wrong, acting in humility, respecting those in authority, but recognizing that our ultimate authority comes from God. When Peter and John were forbidden to preach about Jesus, they replied to the authorities, "We must obey God rather than any human authority" (Acts 5:29 NRSV). One Jewish leader, Gamaliel, who was "held in honor by all the people" (v. 34) then had the courage and humility to say to everyone assembled:

... Let them go! For if their purpose or activity is of human origin, it will fail. But if it is from God, you will not be able to stop these men; you will only find yourselves fighting against God. (Acts 5:38b-39)

We hold the same hope when we work for justice. We may not be spared criticism, or even imprisonment, but if we are truly about our Father's business, his plan will prevail.

Humility also must characterize our approach to those we perceive as the victims of injustice. Compassion demands that we identify with the oppressed, then mutually plan for goals and the means to attain them. We listen and plan *with* people not *for* them.

Irene Schomus, a nurse in Mississippi, tells of her growing identification with the poor:

> I think the tension developed in me during those years [as a hospital nurse] partly because as I became increasingly sensitized to the needs of the poor, I also attended evangelical, Bible-believing, upper-middle class churches in the suburbs. I sensed a dichotomy between my work with the poor and my church community. I believed God calls Christians to be involved with the poor.[8]

So Irene moved to the small town of New Hebron, Mississippi, where she joined a new health-care ministry associated with Voice of Calvary Ministries, an evangelical group committed to racial reconciliation and community development among the poor. She lived in the community she served and joined a local Black church. She grew to love the people with whom she lived and worked.

Not everyone is ready or able to move to rural Mississippi, but there are many means at our disposal to effect change. Some of them require more radical involvement than others. Some ways of doing justice take very little time and effort, but bring great rewards.

Ways of Doing Justice

The first means available to each of us is in *speaking out*. When you become aware of injustice in your work situation or community, appeal to the sense of justice in your colleagues, superiors and local officials. Be careful not to accuse; just present the facts. It could be in quiet one-to-one conversation, an in-service program, teaching a Sunday-school class or addressing a town meeting.

Janet Fuller decided to speak up when a physician ordered an overdose of intravenous morphine for a terminally ill woman. The morphine had been started on the previous shift and the woman, who had been alert, was now nearly stuporous. She had not complained of pain. The only reason Janet could see for giving such a large dose of morphine was to depress her respirations and hasten death. She was able to get the order changed.[9] Florence Nightingale spoke out and changed the entire nursing profession.

An important extension of speaking is *writing*. The power of the written word can be amazing. Arthur Simon, executive director of Bread for the World and brother of Senator Paul Simon, states:

> Expressing our views is important. Based on his experience in Congress, my brother Paul says, "One letter to a member of Congress on a hunger issue saves a life."[10]

He further elaborates the power of letters to members of Congress by telling about when Bread for the World was attempting to promote legislation that would encourage the development of food reserves at the village level in Africa. One particular senator could provide key leadership to get the bill out of committee and onto the floor for a vote, but he was wavering. Bread for the World contacted supporters in the senator's district and asked them to write letters. Later, the senator's aide remarked that he had received a "ton of mail" on the issue. When asked how many letters arrived, he replied, "Twenty." The provision passed the committee with the senator's strong support (p. 13).

We also can write letters to the editors of local papers and nursing journals to express justice concerns. I have even a written letter to the editors of a dictionary when I found a definition of the word *adoption* that presented inaccurate stereotypes. They responded to say it would be changed in the next edition.

Beyond letter writing some nurses can write articles for magazines and journals, or even books, which will provide seed thoughts to inspire others to become involved in issues and needs. When *Spiritual Care: The Nurse's Role* by Sharon Fish and Judith Allen Shelly was first published in 1978, the spiritual dimension of nursing was rarely considered. Today it has become part of nursing curricula in both Christian and secular programs and also the basis for many nursing-research studies, master's theses and doctoral dissertations.

Even writing reports can have a major impact. When nurses keep accurate records of problems that occur repeatedly, action is more likely to be taken. For example, Mary Ann constantly complained to the nursing office about understaffing on her unit, but no additional help was sent. Then she began to write detailed records of the effects of inadequate staffing, including treatments omitted and dangerous situations when call lights could not be answered quickly. After two weeks she submitted the list to her supervisor. Within a week a new RN and an aide were added to the 7-3 shift.

Giving our money, time and abilities is another means of doing justice. Giving money enables those with the time and talents to concentrate on what they do well. You can support world hunger relief agencies, missionaries, crisis pregnancy clinics and other groups that are working for justice. You can give your time by serving on committees and boards, making phone calls, or even stuffing envelopes. Giving your abilities might include volunteering at an inner city clinic or a homeless shelter or, perhaps, taking blood pressures at a senior citizen center.

Participating in effecting change goes one step beyond giving. It could be leaving a well-paying job to work in a poverty-stricken rural health-care center, like Irene Schomus, or even participating in civil disobedience. For example, Lynn believes strongly that abortion should be illegal. She frequently joins pro-life demonstrations and has even been arrested, but she believes that her participation matters.

A key to participation involves creativity. As you look around you and see the needs, what action could correct the situation? Pat saw tremendous need in her church. Too many people were being discharged from hospitals before they could care for themselves at home. Members on special diets were often confused about how to follow the instructions they were quickly given in a doctor's office. Some older people never sent in their Medicare forms because they thought it was "charity" and were too proud to collect. Some members of the senior citizens group were paying thirty-five dollars a week for an office visit to their doctors merely to have their blood pressure checked. Also, the changing neighborhood which surrounded the church had many young families with health problems. At the time Pat was working on her Bachelor of Science in Nursing degree and needed a senior project. She decided to establish a Parish Nurse program in her church as her project. She began routinely visiting each member after a hospital discharge. If a person needed help, Pat would organize volunteers or find the appropriate social service agencies. She set up a series of programs on health topics including nutrition, child care, fitness and cancer screening that drew people from the community and the congregation. She did blood pressure screening at the senior citizens group meetings. Then, Pat talked to each nurse, social worker, physical education teacher and physician from the congregation. She found an eager group of volunteers. A "health cabinet" was formed which assessed the health needs of the congregation and community and planned ways to meet them. Pat's creativity made basic health care more accessible to a large group of needy people.[11]

Political action is another way of attempting to bring justice. The first step to becoming involved in politics is learning about the issues. Professional journals, Christian publications and the local newspaper give constant information about bills before Congress, community and health-care needs and citizen-action groups. As you become informed about the issues, prayerfully decide which ones demand your participation; then pray for wisdom and direction.

Christians have traditionally been suspicious of politics, and many are afraid to become involved. Part of that fear may stem from the realization that often there is not an absolute right and wrong to an issue, or that compromise may be necessary. Theologian Richard John Neuhaus states:

> We do not have a word from the Lord on whether hungry children of the poor should be fed through a food stamp program or through a guaranteed annual income. We do have a word from the

Lord against a system that allows them to go hungry.[12]

Many evangelicals harshly criticized former Surgeon General C. Everett Koop's willingness to compromise to cause change. Yet he probably made more progress in advancing important public health policies than any Surgeon General in recent history. *Christianity Today* quotes *Mademoiselle* magazine as saying:

> Koop, by exercising an agonized compassion for the poor, the wounded and the disenfranchised, has successfully and spectacularly integrated his religious and professional life. He is Christian, but he is not sectarian.[13]

Recently in Pennsylvania a nurse with a clear pro-abortion platform ran for governor. She expected strong endorsement by state nursing organizations. Yet, Christians within those organizations protested and she was not endorsed. Christian nurses cannot afford to sit out the political scene. If we do not provide leadership based on biblical principles of justice and mercy, others will fill the vacuum.

Few nurses are ready to run for governor, but there are more basic steps we can take to begin political action. Obviously, the first step is informed voting. Get to know your candidates; study the issues; look at the voting records of your present legislators; express your views through phone calls, letters, personal contact and in the voting booth. Remember that elected officials are dependent upon your vote to stay in office. They probably will listen carefully to your concerns.

When important issues surface, organize others of like mind to exert influence. You could begin with a letter-writing campaign or form a citizen-action group. Mindy, a Christian nurse in Philadelphia, is taking her political interest one step further. She is taking a leave of absence from her nursing position to go to Washington, D.C., to lobby for health-care issues.

Entering the political ring may not be for you, but one means of doing justice is open to—and required of—each of us as Christians. We must be committed to *praying* for those who are doing justice and for those who are victims of injustice. As we seriously engage in the work of prayer—fasting, mourning and lamenting over the injustice that surrounds us—the Lord will open our eyes and our hearts to his role for each of us in the work of his kingdom.

Finally, we may find ourselves *suffering* for the cause of justice. "Blowing the whistle" on an evil situation may cost you your job. Taking a stand may result in demotion or loss of prestige. Ellen refused to participate in New Age therapies begun in her psychiatric hospital. She was soon demoted from head nurse to staff nurse and assigned to the geriatric unit where the new therapies were not used.

Identifying with the poor may lead you to ". . . sell your possessions and give to the poor" (Mt 19:21). Ann Connor, a nursing instructor in Georgia, and her husband did just that. They bought a large house and turned it into a shelter for the homeless and an intentional Christian community. But Ann doesn't focus on the suffering. She focuses on the blessing.[14]

The apostle Peter tells us:

Dear friends, do not be surprised at the painful trial you are suffering, as though something strange were happening to you. But rejoice that you participate in the sufferings of Christ, so that you may be overjoyed when his glory is revealed. (1 Pet 4:12-13)

Sometimes that glory is revealed in victories for justice and mercy right away. Sometimes we face a long struggle, and sometimes we must wait for the kingdom to come fully before we see injustice ended.

In the process of doing justice the Christian community is essential. We need the resources of the entire body of Christ to recognize and confront injustice in our world. We need each other to stay humble and to keep us from becoming "Lone Rangers" riding out on white horses to conquer evil single-handedly. We need one another's perspective to see all sides of an issue and to consider the best way to approach problems. We need the physical, emotional and spiritual support of the Christian community when we meet opposition and failure. Prayer and

Bible study give us the solid foundation necessary to go out into the world as "salt" and "light" in the name of Jesus Christ (Mt 5:13-16).

Discussion Questions

Context for Discussion: Matthew 23:23

a. What should be the relationship between spirituality and action?

b. How does Jesus view personal piety which does not result in justice and mercy?

Describe a situation where you have recently seen injustice.

Discuss the following questions as they relate to the situation.

1. What "health rights" does each person have in this setting? Consider requirements for life, access to basic services and access to accurate information.

2. If justice does not prevail (persons are not receiving their rights) identify *which persons* are being deprived.

3. Identify sources of the injustice. Consider both general, human causes and specific, structural causes.

4. What power do you have to make the situation more just?

10

CHRISTIAN NURSING IN A SECULAR PROFESSION

Arlene B. Miller

*B*y now it should be obvious that we are writing to Christian nurses. But how does all this apply to everyday life in nursing? We've all been well indoctrinated with the value-neutral approach for such a public profession as nursing. The voices of fellow nurses ring in our heads saying, "That's how you see it, but I see it differently," or "You have no right to force your values on other people." We are also aware that other health workers and patients with whom we work come from diverse cultural and religious backgrounds. How, then, can we write a book for nurses that advocates specifically Christian values for nursing? Doesn't such an attitude promote intolerance and even bigotry within a profession that needs all the unity it can inspire? Aren't we merely increasing the pressure sensitive nurses already experience, in a harried and stressful environment, by suggesting that religious values are not only for our private lives but for our public work life as well?

Christians in the Larger Society

Such questions are as old as Christianity itself, and the roots of them are deep within the history of God's people. Put succinctly, the issue becomes, "How are the followers of God to relate to those around them who do not follow him as he has revealed himself in the history of Israel, in Jesus Christ and in Scripture?" The answers—from the beginnings of the early church in the pagan Roman Empire to modern times—have varied in response to the attitude of the larger society toward them. Christians have been persecuted minorities in hostile societies and, in turn, Christians when in the majority have sometimes been the persecutors of minorities.

When Christianity became the "official" religion of the Roman Empire (following the conversion of Emperor Constantine), the structures of the church became the societal glue replacing the crumbling supports of the empire. Church and state became one and the same. For the nearly twelve centuries that this arrangement prevailed, becoming a baptized Christian and a citizen was synonymous. The question of how European Christians should relate to non-Christians was primarily directed toward Jews and Muslims, not one's fellow citizens, for all were considered Christian. The problem was, of course, that many so-called Christians led lives that were anything but Christian.

In the sixteenth century large numbers of European Christians challenged this understanding of church and government, many of them paying with their lives. They were called radical Reformers, and they were indeed too radical for the so-called magisterial Reformers like Luther, Calvin and Zwingli—who still held to the unity, or at least alliance, of civil government and the church. The fear of course was anarchy—anarchy in belief and anarchy in actions. But the seeds of ideas were sown and from them came the now commonly accepted doctrine of separation of church and state.

Today the attitudes of Christians toward the larger society range all the way from physical separation and living apart in separate communities (like the Amish or the Bruderhof communities) to identifying with the larger society on the basis of a "civil religion."[1] Those who separate themselves see the role of the church as witnessing to society what life in the kingdom of heaven is like rather than trying to make the larger society Christian. They do not attempt to influence legislation by direct political action. Instead they see the church as an alternative society, following Jesus in its life together. Anyone who wants to follow Jesus in this way is welcome to join with them. Their motives have often been questioned by those who see their separation as a form of escapism or a futile endeavor in utopianism. While such motives may be present, they are secondary to the conviction that their life in community is to challenge the corrupted structures of the surrounding culture.

On the other hand, those Christians who choose to identify with the culture around them must struggle with the secularism and religious pluralism. *Secularism* prevails because we do not have any officially sanctioned religion. Increasingly, any references to religion in public life are being challenged. *Religious pluralism* flourishes at the same time because, although religion is relegated to one's private life, a vigorous interest in spiritual matters continues. A growing number of new spiritualities attest to this interest.

Much is the same as in the first century, when Jesus left behind a small group of disciples, except that now all religions, including Christianity, are viewed as non-universal and non-rational. The professional community considers reason, not faith, to be the means of discovering those universal rules accepted by all rational people. They see religion as *only* a personal and sociological phenomenon. Public appeals to God's authority are reduced to "you have your understanding and I have mine." To most people God is merely an idea—perhaps a helpful idea, but only an idea nevertheless.

Christians in the Nursing Profession

This brief excursion into church history brings us to the pressing concerns of Christian nurses who are wondering how Christian values relate to their work. Both the profession itself and most of the institutions and agencies where nurses work are secular in orientation. Over the last decades nursing leaders have insisted that nursing can no longer be viewed as a "calling" because of that term's religious implications. Rather, nursing must be considered a career for educated, skilled persons who are reimbursed at a level comparable to their education and skill. Because nursing is a secular profession, the values it espouses are expected to be based not upon religion but on tradition, civil laws and the results of scientific inquiry—not religion. Nursing ethics are based on the assumption that the discipline of ethics can stand alone. The nurse's religion, while valuable to her personally, cannot be granted universal validity.[2]

Beyond the profession of nursing itself most health-care institutions in America are *non-sectarian.* Even church-related institutions are often secular at the practical level of day-to-day functioning. Most nurses have heard at least one warning from administration concerning proselytizing patients. Several years ago a chain of for-profit hospitals decided to prohibit clergy from visiting patients in the hospital unless the patient specifically requested them.

Christian nurse educators in secular educational institutions, especially those supported by tax monies, are told to refrain from advocating any specific religious position. Those faculty members who teach courses relating to spiritual care must either present spirituality as an abstract generic concept or as comparative religion. Some merely teach emotional support as spiritual care. However, some of the new "spiritual" theories of nursing gain acceptance by defining spiritual concepts in scientific terminology.

Despite the public disavowal of religion in nursing, spirituality is thriving in the private lives of patients and health-care workers. In many hospitals, especially in urban areas, Christian nurses often find themselves working with other staff who espouse a variety of religions, cults or no religion at all. Some hospitals hire nurses from other countries, nurses who bring their religions with them. Christians working in certain areas of North America may encounter members of the Native American Church who engage in peyote worship. But even middle-American culture is giving birth to a variety of new spiritualities. Recent nursing modalities claim to channel cosmic energy to heal patients. New Age advocates carry crystals to harmonize bad vibrations and calm either themselves or fellow workers. I once worked with a nurse who claimed to be a witch. Seeing the multiplicity of religions and spiritualities can make us more appreciative of hospital policies that prevent nurses from proselytizing.

How, then, are Christian nurses to practice their profession in this kind of world? Christians are called neither to total isolation from the surrounding culture nor to complete identification with it. Instead, Jesus sends us to live *in* without being *of* the world. We can learn something both from those Christians who feel called to separate themselves and from those who identify with the society around them. Remember the Hebrews who were carried captive from Judah to Babylon and how they were called by God to live in that foreign country. Can we learn from those ancient followers of God who learned how to be both in and not of the world around them? What does this story from our tradition say to us today? Let us see.

Learning from History

We begin the story around 600 years before Christ. The Babylonian

Empire was expanding by conquering the territory ruled over by other kings. As part of its policy of subjugating the surrounding peoples, Babylonia carried some citizens from these countries into Babylon. Such policies produced a "brain drain" from the conquered nations. The Babylonians took only the best minds and skills to help build their expanding empire.

Jeremiah, one of God's faithful prophets, wrote a letter from Judah to Hebrew leaders exiled in Babylon with the following advice:

This is what the LORD Almighty, the God of Israel, says to all those I carried into exile from Jerusalem to Babylon: "Build houses and settle down; plant gardens and eat what they produce. Marry and have sons and daughters; find wives for your sons and give your daughters in marriage, so that they too may have sons and daughters. Increase in number there; do not decrease. Also, seek the peace and prosperity of the city to which I have carried you into exile. Pray to the LORD for it, because if it prospers, you too will prosper. (Jer 29:4-7)

Among the captives were some handsome, fit and bright young men brought from the Jewish court in Jerusalem to serve in the government of the Babylonian king. Daniel and his friends, Hananiah, Mishael and Azariah, enrolled in a three-year program to learn the language and literature of the Babylonians (Dan 1:1-5). The school headmaster gave them each a Babylonian name that incorporated references to Babylonian deities. They apparently accepted these names without any fuss. No doubt the names were for official use and privately the four friends called each other by their Hebrew names.

The curriculum of the school was another matter. Learning the language was certainly a pragmatic necessity if they were to carry on day-to-day government business, but they were also required to study the Babylonian literature used by the court wise men. How could a Hebrew who worshiped the one true God and was schooled in the teachings of Moses study the religion of the Sumerians and Babylonians? Many gods inhabited this religion. Each was placed on a divine scale that ranged from major deities to demons. Furthermore, the court wise men needed to know the ways of magic, sorcery, charms and astrology—all strictly forbidden by the God of Daniel, Hananiah, Mishael and Azariah.

There is no hint in the book of Daniel that they refused to study this literature. Later in the book we discover that the elaborate dream manuals proved to be useless when the distraught king could not remember his troublesome dream. Unable to look up the dream which best corresponded to the king's, Daniel put the reputation of Israel's God on the line by promising that he would reveal both the dream and the meaning.

Several Bible commentators suggest that the Hebrews studied this religion and the magical practices accompanying it so they could prove the superiority of the one God of Israel to the Babylonian pantheon. Only as they understood the thinking of their captors could they speak to them of the one true God. They were truly crosscultural missionaries.

It will be helpful here to jump briefly to the end of Daniel's story. He lived most of his life as a royal advisor in the court of Babylon. While still in Judah, he had seen the fall of the Assyrian Empire as Babylon extended its power, and in the closing days of his life Babylon itself fell under the domination of Persia (modern-day Iran). It was under the Persian king that Daniel's enemies hatched a plot to trap Daniel, and they had him thrown into a den of lions for continuing his lifelong habit of daily prayer (Dan 6). He was a survivor, not by his own designs, scheming and compromising of principle, but because God chose to use him in that way.

How did these young Hebrews keep from becoming totally assimilated into the culture and religion of their new country? At least two reasons seem evident: they knew the Scriptures, and they knew where to drive their stakes down deeply. The prophets Isaiah, Jeremiah, Zephaniah and Habakkuk had been preparing the Hebrews for the coming captivity through warnings, assurances of God's faithfulness and promises that they would return to the Promised Land. The captives were told to settle in their new country, but they were not to lose their identity as Hebrews. Daniel and his friends absorbed the message of these faithful prophets of God. They knew they were resident aliens. That was to be their status. The test of their identity came soon enough.

That test had to do with food, one of the most basic requirements for life. It seems strange on the face of it that these young men so readily plunged into the study of Babylonian religion and magic, even accepting Babylonian names. Perhaps Daniel had the good sense to know that the so-called gods to which the names referred were really no gods at all. Making a fuss was not worth it. But food was a different story! Jewish food laws have been instrumental in maintaining the unique identity of the Hebrew people throughout their history. It was here that Daniel and his three friends took their stand.

The king provided food for the men in his school from the royal kitchens. It was the best of meat and drink and may have been ceremonially offered to one of the gods prior to being served. Daniel and his friends didn't want to eat it. Commentators suggest several reasons why this became their sticking point, but all the Scripture says is that Daniel believed he would be defiled if he ate that food. He asked the school steward to give them vegetables and water that did not come from the royal kitchens. Kosher food laws, or the fact that it was offered to the gods first, may have been behind Daniel's reasoning. Commentator Joyce Baldwin suggests that eating food from another's table in that culture implied a commitment of allegiance to the host.[3] Whatever the reason, this was the issue of Hebrew identity for Daniel and his friends.

Daniel asked the school superintendent (who favored Daniel) for permission to refuse the food. The superintendent denied his request, fearing that the Hebrews would not look as healthy as the others, inciting the king's wrath. Daniel persisted with the attendant assigned to them. "Give us a ten-day trial," he argued, "and then make your decision as to whether or not we appear to be less healthy." Perhaps the attendant connived with the superintendent to exchange the vegetables and water of his own diet for the rich foods, thus benefiting himself and ensuring that the secret would be kept.[4] Of course, we know from this often-told Sunday-school story that indeed the health of Daniel and his friends flourished, and after the ten-day trial the arrangement became permanent. Their faithfulness to God in this instance strengthened their character and prepared them for more difficult situations to come.[5]

The four young Hebrews distinguished themselves in the school and completed their course of study with honors. Actually, it is not correct to say that they did it themselves. Scripture is quite clear that God had a lot to do with their success: "To these four young men God gave knowledge and understanding of all kinds of literature and learning. And Daniel could understand visions and dreams of all kinds" (Dan 1:17).

King Nebuchadnezzar had the graduates presented to him. After talking with them all he found none equal to Daniel, Hananiah, Mishael and Azariah. "In every matter of wisdom and understanding about which the king questioned them, he found them ten times better than all the magicians and enchanters in his whole kingdom" (Dan 1:20). Each of them was given a government appointment, Daniel in the court of the king and his three friends in an outlying province.

The first six chapters of Daniel are stories from the lives of Daniel and his three Hebrew friends. Children who have grown up in Sunday school or have heard bedtime Bible stories know them well: Daniel and his friends appealing to the God of heaven for help in interpreting the forgotten dream of Nebuchadnezzar; the refusal of the Hebrews to bow before the king's image and their subsequent deliverance out of the fiery furnace (Dan 3); the dramatic intervention of God in the life of Nebuchadnezzar to bring him to submission (Dan 4); Daniel insisting before the doomed Belshazzar that the Most High God rules in the kingdoms of men and was still giving him, Belshazzar, an opportunity to repent (Dan 5); and God delivering Daniel from the den of lions (Dan 6).

In the second part of the book of Daniel we read the reports of Daniel's visions: visions of the unseen spiritual struggles behind the affairs of the world, visions of God's purposes for and control of human history and visions that incorporated all the nations of the world into the realm of God's concern. Both the stories and the visions with their different points of view are keys to the theological significance of the book of Daniel.

Daniel's Relevance to Nursing
How, then, does this story from so long ago instruct nurses today? Not only is it ancient, but a story of captives from Judah working in the government of a pagan nation seems unrelated to the life of nurses in high-tech health-care settings struggling to live out Christian values. But is it really?

Daniel has inspired young Christians, especially those in cultures hostile to their faith, to remain faithful to God and to retain their identity in the face of pressures to conform. Christian nurses living in North America who earlier may have considered themselves living in a Christian society can do so no longer. Many Christian nurses are beginning to feel in the minority when working in units where the jokes of other staff are crude, at best, and evil at worst, or where most turn a blind eye to the pilfering of supplies. The line from the Sunday-school song—"Dare to be a Daniel, dare to stand alone"—can still encourage us when we feel alone in hostile territory. Let us reflect more specifically how Daniel's story can help us in a secular profession.

Daniel Put God's Honor First

In a culture that values power, prestige and economic success the traditional values that motivate most nurses (care, compassion and service) are devalued. From a Christian perspective, current recruitment attempts that focus on salary, benefits, prestige and independence of nurses are counterproductive for nursing. Nurses should be paid a fair wage, be given more humane schedules and be respected for their knowledge and expertise; however, the services that nurses provide can never be glamorous. Even the stimulation of high-tech settings cannot remove nurses from bodies that smell, fall and die. A nursing student recently said to me, "Nursing is humiliating!" I agreed with her. Recent movements of nurses into expanded roles, even though needed and giving more autonomy, do not solve the problems of nurses working in short-staffed hospitals, nursing homes, and home-health agencies. A director of nursing worries about the reduced number of graduates and fears that the future will increasingly bring mere technicians who narrowly define their work and focus primarily on benefits and salary. High-school guidance counselors direct bright young students into medicine or other traditionally male-dominated fields because they see nursing as menial work.

What, then, will it take to interest capable young men and women in entering nursing? What will it take to keep practicing nurses from leaving the profession? Certainly they must be persons of character. They must be persons who can stand against false cultural values because their goal is to follow the call of God and to honor him with their lives. They must be women and men who have responded to the call of Jesus, "Come, follow me."

Beyond the issue of attracting capable women and men to nursing as a calling is how we find our place within the profession. For many climbing the professional ladder has become the way for self-validation. When this becomes the driving force behind upward movement, many people take positions, not because they have the strengths for them, but because the position is another upward step. Promotion of self in this way leads to manipulating and using others. For Christians such upward movement should come out of God's call to serve and to use one's God-given gifts. Again, the motive is to put God's honor first.

Daniel Knew the Scriptures

Christian nurses must know the Bible—both the content of the Scriptures and how to apply them to their lives. We need to be theologians as well. We need not be theological scholars, but we should at least understand major theological themes. Theology provides an overall picture of the biblical message, enabling us to more fully grasp each individual passage.

Theology applies to Christian witness as well, because it helps us to say more clearly what we have to say about God. The same thing can be said for dealing with the myriad of spiritualities and religions that surround us in today's world. Learning from Christian thinkers throughout the history of the church will help us immensely. Much of their work grew from wrestling with what the Scriptures taught about the unorthodox teaching that they faced. Almost every "new" religion or spiritual teaching has appeared before in another guise.

Nursing theories are increasingly sophisticated, and some of them are providing useful ways of thinking about nursing. Many of them reflect a naturalistic perspective, while others incorporate more easily into a Christian perspective. But a new flood of "spiritual" theories are powerfully influencing and shaping nursing education and practice. Such theories reflect a God-created need for persons to go beyond the material level of life. They also reflect human response to the spiritual aspect of being human. It will take nurses who know the Scriptures and theology to provide the Christian critique of these theories. Where are the Christian nursing theories?

Likewise, the Scriptures should provide the filter through which

Christian nurses view the agendas and goals of nursing organizations. Do they reflect Christian values that we can endorse? The Scriptures provide a way of thinking about the problems of life and death that bombard us in caring for patients. They provide the insight for dealing with coworkers. Serious Bible study and reading of Christian theologians should characterize the Christian nurse who wants to retain a Christian identity and respond as a Christian to issues in nursing.

Daniel Knew the Pagan Culture

We need to know the world in which we work. For each of us that world may be quite different. Some of us should study the beliefs and thinking of our patients and coworkers in order to engage them in sensitive and knowledgeable conversation about God. Some of us need to study current nursing theories, knowing what parts of them we can support as Christians and where true heresy is being introduced. Some of us need to know the world of politics from institutional to government levels so that we can involve ourselves effectively. All of us need to know the language of the culture around us even if it is to refrain from speaking it. Such cultural involvement in nursing that will engage us in the wider culture for nursing is but a mirror of the world in which we live, reflecting its values and viewpoint.

Daniel Influenced the Culture

All of us have been given moral power that drives and guides our use of other forms of power that have been entrusted to us. Nurses can influence nursing and the health-care system. But too often we retreat from engagement, excusing ourselves because we see our influence as too small to make a difference. Just as God called Daniel in a foreign pagan court to bear witness to him, so we are called into our places of work and influence to bear witness to him there.

Daniel Earned Both Respect and Fear

Lest we think that retaining our Christian identity will bring us instant respect and recognition, let us think again. Daniel was not in the favor of the first two monarchs under whom he worked, and it was only grudgingly that they gave him honor when they recognized that it was the power and wisdom of his God that saved the day. Whenever a crisis erupted in the court, Daniel had to be called, giving us the impression that he might not have always been there. Perhaps those in the court were actually more comfortable when he wasn't there with his moral rectitude. More than one nurse has been harassed for refusing to use crude language, or for not going to the bar for long hours after work. These issues gnaw at our personal equanimity. Today, there are many angry people in nursing fighting for a variety of issues: unionization, abortion rights for adolescents, distribution of contraceptives in schools, recognition of gay and lesbian lifestyles. Whatever position we take on these and many other like issues, Christian nurses cannot pretend that these are value-neutral concerns. Insisting that the moral issues be recognized will bring us into inevitable conflict.

Daniel Remained Free

For each nurse there will come the place to drive down the stake in order to maintain an open Christian identity. Networking, the current buzz word for cultivating the personal loyalties of people in one's institution or profession, can become a hard master, demanding reciprocal back scratching. Moral authority for nurses is multifaceted, ranging from the client and the physician to the institution and the profession. For Christian nurses, the ultimate authority remains God himself and our understanding of his moral character.

Where the test will come for each of us will vary, but each of us will face at least one place where our very identity as Christ-followers will be called into question. It is here that we echo the words of Peter, "We must obey God rather than any human authority" (Acts 5:29 NRSV). The consequences may be social isolation, lack of promotion (or even demotion), loss of work or lack of prestige. On the other hand, we may be promoted, as Daniel was, to greater responsibilities. The outcome is in God's hands. The words of Daniel's friends who were threatened with death in a fiery furnace instruct us:

O Nebuchadnezzar, we do not need to defend ourselves before you in this matter. If we are thrown into the blazing furnace, the God we serve is able to save us from it, and he will rescue us from your hand, O king. But even if he does not, we want you to know, O king, that we will not serve your gods or worship the image of gold you have set up. (Dan 3:16-18)

Daniel Turned to Believing Friends

Christian nurses need to hold each other accountable and support one another. It was on his friends that Daniel called after his audacious offer to recount and interpret the king's forgotten dream. It is to fellow Christian nurses we go to wrestle through tough decisions, to pray for situations on our clinical units and to help us think creatively about solutions for the unique problems in our place in nursing. Many Christian nurses have experienced miraculous changes in their attitudes and those of their colleagues through praying consistently with a friend. Finding a network of Christian nurses with similar interests is essential.

Daniel Prayed Routinely

It was Daniel's prayer life that finally got him thrown into a den of lions as an old man. It was also this day-after-day praying that kept him strong and faithful to God all those years in the pagan courts of power. I wonder what he prayed about? Certainly there were those ritual prayers, which every Jew prayed daily. But certainly he prayed about all the other concerns in his life, explaining the dreams of the kings, confessing the sins of his fellow Hebrews (Dan 9:4-19). What would happen if we confessed the sins of nursing? Perhaps God would give us wisdom for the multitude of problems that we face.

Daniel Knew God Would Deal with Suffering

The stories in Daniel are cliffhangers. They pose a terrible crisis in which God's honor is at stake. Daniel and his friends put their lives on the line only to be saved in the end. But Daniel knew that it wouldn't always be like that, and in the visions he saw evil triumphing and good people suffering. Christian nurses find it the same. Women and children are abused. Drug dealers live extravagantly while young people are ensnared and ruined by their wares. The homeless wander in and out the health-care system, receiving inadequate care and no follow-up. People suffer and die.

Our culture has no way to deal with evil and suffering. The increasing openness to suicide as a way to deal with suffering reflects this void. New spiritualities trivialize death by speaking of it romantically as the next stage of growth. Socially sensitive people burn themselves out trying to reform the system which they find terribly resistant to reform. Christians know very well that evil and suffering are real and that mere good intentions and hard work will not change them. They know that Scripture speaks of the secret power of lawlessness at work in the world. They also know that evil is being restrained by God and that things are not as bad as they could be. And Christians know that the Lord Jesus will overthrow the lawless one by the breath of his mouth and the splendor of his coming (2 Thess 2:7-8). They know that for now we are to stand firm, to hold to Christian teachings and to encourage one another (2 Thess 2:13-16).

Daniel Trusted God

We are creatures of faith, and we must place our faith in someone or something. Here I mean faith, not primarily as a system of belief, but the foundation on which our lives are built. God calls us to always put our faith in him alone. Christian nurses, wherever they are employed, constantly need to monitor where their faith is placed. In other words, what are the false gods that seduce us today? Professionalism? Education? Position? Power? Financial security? The "network"? Knowledge? Expertise? Political savvy? Autonomy? Better nursing theory? Research? Better practice models? Our wits? Survival? None of these things is wrong in and of itself when placed within a larger frame of reference. But when these goals become gods, they prove false, and we need to search for the true God, Jesus Christ. Most tragically, we commit spiritual adultery by turning away from the One True God. He is the God who sees the past and the future as well as the present—the God of all hope.

Hope is what we need today in nursing. It is in short supply! Hope arises from knowing God, the One True God. The visions of Daniel are full of the power of evil and of suffering for God's people. But there are promises scattered throughout that God, himself, would strengthen those who knew him and purify them, even if they stumble. Finally, Daniel was told:

> But at that time your people—everyone whose name is found written in the book—will be delivered. Multitudes who sleep in the dust of the earth will awake: some to everlasting life, others to shame and everlasting contempt. Those who are wise will shine like the brightness of the heavens, and those who lead many to righteousness, like the stars for ever and ever. (Dan 12:1b-3)

Leading many to righteousness: that is being wise; that is bringing hope. Trust God and lead many to righteousness. Daniel did it in the court of a pagan king. Christian nurses are called to do the same in a secular profession.

Discussion Questions

Context for Discussion: 1 Corinthians 16:13

a. This verse gives five admonitions to the church at Corinth. List and define them.

b. Discuss some specific ways you can apply these admonitions to your work situation.

Review the principles Daniel followed while living in Babylon. How could you apply each principle to your own situation?

1. Daniel put the honor of God before anything else. In what areas might you be compromising the honor of God? What do you plan to do about it?

2. Daniel knew the Scriptures. How can you learn more from and about the Bible? Set some specific goals.

3. Daniel knew the pagan culture. How can you learn more about your own culture? Develop a plan.

4. Daniel was involved in and influenced the culture. Think of at least one way you can influence nursing for Jesus Christ.

5. Daniel earned both the respect and fear of those around him. In what ways can you earn the respect of your colleagues?

6. Daniel remained free where his loyalty to God was at stake. What other loyalties compete with your faithfulness to God? What steps can you take to overcome them?

7. Daniel sought the support and companionship of Christian friends. Where do you find your Christian support network? If it is presently inadequate, what steps will you take to develop one?

8. Daniel disciplined himself with routine prayer. Describe your current prayer practices. How can you improve in this area?

9. Daniel understood that God would ultimately deal with suffering. In what ways do you see or experience suffering? How does knowing God is in control give you hope?

10. Daniel trusted God. What causes you the most anxiety? What would it mean for you to trust God in that situation?

APPENDIX A:
A DICTIONARY OF CHRISTIAN VALUES
Judith Allen Shelly

altruism—Altruism is working for the good of other persons. For the Christian it is based on God's love and extended to everyone, including enemies (Mt 5:44), strangers (Heb 13:2) and outcasts (Jas 1:27). Jesus carried altruism to the ultimate by dying for humankind, and instructed his followers to be willing to do the same (Jn 15:12-13). Altruism is contrary to human nature, but altruistic acts can be highly satisfying and, therefore, may stem from hidden egoism. The personal satisfaction from altruism has been a strong motivating factor for nurses.

ambition—The strong desire to achieve or succeed is an important character trait in leaders, yet most Christians seem to feel uncomfortable with ambition. The Bible presents a delicate balance between the need to strive toward a goal (1 Cor 9:24; 1 Tim 4:11) and the need to wait patiently for God to act (Is 40:31; Heb 6:15). Paul gives the proper context for Christian ambition when he argues passionately, listing his worldly credentials and achievements in order to establish his authority with the Corinthian church (2 Cor 10-12). Philippians 2:3 tells us that we are to "do nothing of *selfish* ambition." Determined, goal-directed behavior is appropriate when working toward God's aims (1 Cor 14:12; Mt 6:33; 2 Tim 4:2; Heb 11:33-34), but inappropriate when used for selfish pursuits.

assertiveness—Not only were God's servants in the Bible strongly assertive, they advocated assertiveness. However, it was a qualified assertiveness. The prophets, patriarchs, apostles and Jesus had godly motives and just methods. The goal of their assertiveness was to glorify God. See Nehemiah 13; Acts 4:1-31; 2 Cor 10; 1 Pet 2; Mt 18:15-17; 1 Tim 5:1-2; 1 Pet 5:5-11; Eph 4:15-32.

authority—For the Christian, the ultimate authority is God (Ex 2:1-6; Eph 1:15-23), but God delegates authority to people. Those with authority are to use it responsibly (Gen 45:1-8; Ex 3:7-10; Ps 72; Mt 28:18; Luke 10:17-20; 1 Pet. 5:1-4). Christians are to respect human authorities (Rom 13:1; Eph 6:1-9; 1 Tim 5:17; 1 Pet 5:5), except when their commands conflict with God's authority (Dan 3:16-18; Acts 5:29; 1 Pet 5:8-9).

autonomy—Autonomy, in its full sense, is not possible within the Christian world view, for persons must either be servants of God or slaves to sin. However, all persons have a God-given right and responsibility to make choices about lifestyle and values (Deut 30:19-20; Josh 24:14-15; Lk 10:42). Jesus respected the limited autonomy of persons by allowing them to refuse his salvation (Mt 19:20-22).

beneficence—Doing good (beneficence) characterized Jesus' ministry (Acts 10:38). It is rewarded by God (Rom 2:10). God created us to do good works, and we are enabled to do them by grace through faith (Eph 2:10). Almost all ethical theories and religions teach the importance of beneficence. See also *altruism* and *love*.

chastity—Confinement of sexual intercourse to the marriage relationship is a virtue commanded throughout the Bible (Ex 20:14; Deut 5:18; Prov 5:1-23; 7:24-27; Lk 18:20; 1 Cor 6:9-11; Gal 5:16-21). Those who violated God's standards for sexual purity brought judgment upon themselves and often created serious problems for others (Gen 16; cf. Gal 4:21-26; 2 Sam 11:2-27; 12:1-15; Ezek 16:35-43; 1 Cor 10:6-11). Jesus raised chastity to a new level, including thoughts as well as actions, and remarriage after divorce (Mt 5:27-32). Jesus also made it clear that a person who repents of unchastity will be forgiven (Lk 7:36-48; Jn 4:7-42; 8:1-11). The early church had many members who had formerly lived in unchastity, but radically changed their lifestyles upon coming to faith (1 Cor 6:9-11; Gal 5:16-24; Eph 2:1-5; Col 3:5-10; Heb 10:22; 1 Pet 3:21). For some church members unchastity continued to be a problem and was a matter for serious church discipline (1 Cor 5:1-5; Eph 5:3). A relationship of sexual faithfulness in marriage is an illustration of God's faithfulness to his people (Hos; Eph 5:31-33).

compassion—Jesus taught the importance of compassion in the parable of the Good Samaritan (Lk 10:29-37). Compassion is a character trait of God which was clearly demonstrated by Jesus (Mt 9:36; 14:14; 15:32). Christians are expected to "put on" the virtue of compassion (Col 3:12), which involves feeling sympathy for another, leading to acts of beneficence.

competence—God expects us to seek knowledge which prepares us for our work (Prov 4:14; 15:14), to be skilled at our jobs (Ps 78:72; Jer 9:17; 1 Cor 3:10), and to "present yourself to God as one approved, a workman who has no need to be ashamed, rightly handling the word of truth" (2 Tim 2:15). Christians are enjoined, "Whatever your task, put yourselves into it, as done for the Lord and not for your masters" (Col 3:23 NRSV). While competence is important and may give us greater influence (Prov 22:29), the Lord has a way of choosing people who may not seem competent to do his work (1 Cor 1:29-31), so we must be careful when setting standards of competence for ourselves or for others. Ultimately, our confidence and sufficiency must come from God, not human achievements (2 Cor 3:3-5).

confidentiality—"He who goes about as a talebearer reveals secrets, but he who is trustworthy in spirit keeps a thing hidden" (Prov 11:13). Confidentiality is important for the Christian, and the Bible speaks strongly against gossip (Prov 20:19; Rom 1:29; 1 Tim 5:13). Jesus required confidentiality of some people whom he healed (Mk 1:44; Lk 5:14). Rahab, the prostitute, was praised for her ability to keep confidences during a covert operation (Jos 2:1-24; Heb 11:31; Jas 2:25). However, confidentiality can sometimes create an ethical dilemma when withholding confidential information might cause harm to other persons (e.g., when a spouse is not told the diagnosis of a sexually transmitted disease). Proverbs 25:9 gives helpful advice: "Argue your case with your neighbor himself, and do not disclose another's secret." The Bible does not seem to allow for the breaking of confidences, but provides us with the hope that God will ultimately reveal any harmful secrets (Eccles 12:14; Mt 10:26).

cost-effectiveness—Throughout history in various cultures frugality has been seen as a virtue and a guide for rational decision-making. Today frugality is often couched in the language of "cost-effectiveness." The Bible, while teaching that we must be good stewards of material gifts (Gen 1:26; Mt 25:14-28;

Lk 12:42-44; 16:1-12), emphasizes generosity and an open sharing of the gifts God has given with others in need (see *generosity* and *hospitality*). Paying too much attention to personal finances is seen as a form of idolatry (Lk 16:13-15). God is the owner of everything on the earth; we are merely entrusted with its just distribution (Ps 24:1; 50:12; Hag 2:6:-9; Acts 2:44; 4:32; Rom 12:8; 2 Cor 8:13-15; 9:6-15).

courage—Plato saw courage as one of the cardinal virtues (along with wisdom, justice and temperance). Aristotle and the Stoics further developed the concept and influenced the early church, which saw courage as a virtue in the face of martyrdom. The Greeks and the Old Testament viewed courage as fearless bravery on the battlefield (Judges, Samuel, Chronicles). The concept is strikingly absent from the New Testament (the only reference using the Greek word *tharsos* is Acts 28:15). Other references translated "courage" imply not the Stoic sense of fortitude, but a steadfastness in faith (1 Cor 16:13; 2 Cor 5:6; 1 Thes 2:2; Heb 12:5).

credulity—Unquestioning belief is a virtue only when applied to our relationship with God (Mk 1:15; 9:23-24; Jn 1:7; 11:25; 12:44; 14:1; Acts 16:31). 1 Cor 13:7 seems to imply that believing all things is an expression of love; however, that belief must be tempered with discernment, for we are to be "wise as serpents and innocent as doves" (Mt 10:16; Rom 16:18-20). We must guard against deception (Col 2:8).

discernment—The ability to discern good from evil is a mark of spiritual maturity (Heb 5:14; 1 Cor 2:14; Phil 1:9-10). Lack of discernment brings God's disfavor (Is 27:11; 44:18-19; 1 Cor 11: 29).

duty—While certain responsibilities are presented as duties in the New Testament (Lk 17:10; Rom 15:27 in KJV; 1 Tim 5:4), the primary Christian motivation for ethical behavior is not duty or law, but love (Mt 22:37-39; Lk 10:27-37; 1 Jn 3:14-18).

education—Education is useful and important, but never an end in itself, or an absolute requirement for leadership positions. The author of Ecclesiastes relates his career as a scholar, then concludes, "The sayings of the wise are like goads, and like nails firmly fixed are the collected sayings which are given by one Shepherd. My son, beware of anything beyond these. Of making many books there is no end, and much study is a weariness of the flesh" (Eccles 12:11-12). The apostle Paul did not hesitate to list his academic credentials to establish his credibility (Acts 22:3), but he also considered his worldly accomplishments something not worth boasting about (2 Cor 17-18). Paul wrote to Timothy about the importance of teaching others what he had learned (2 Tim 2:2). Jesus spent three years educating the disciples, but most of them began as uneducated working men. The Bible emphasizes that true wisdom comes from God (Ps 111:10; Lk 21:14; Jas 1:5). We must guard against becoming overly impressed with our knowledge, for it is imperfect (1 Cor 8:1-2; 13:9).

efficiency—God is efficient in his work. He spoke and the world was created (Gen 1 & 2). However, when dealing with people, efficiency is seldom God's top priority; he is more concerned with human relationships and providing opportunity for spiritual growth (2 Pet 3:8-9; Ps 90:4). The book of Proverbs criticizes the inefficient sluggard (Prov 6:6; 13:4; 21:25; 26:15-16), and several Bible passages give instructions for efficient government and division of labor (Ex 18:17; Josh 23:1-4; Neh 2—6; Acts 6:1-6). Efficiency is necessary for the smooth operation of a large organization or mechanical functions, but human needs and problems take priority when a nurse must choose between efficiency and compassion.

encouragement—The gospel provides great encouragement to the Christian (Rom 15:4; Phil 2:1; Heb 6:18) and we are to encourage one another with the hope it provides (1 Thess 5:11-14; Rom 1:12; Heb 10:25). Through Christ we are able to encourage others who are disillusioned and suffering.

equality—While human beings are not equal in ability, appearance or achievement (2 Cor 8:7), we are all equal before God (Mk 12:14; Gal 3:28). We are all created in God's image (Gen 1:26), we have all sinned and fallen short of God's glory (Rom 3:22b-23), we are all justified by grace through faith (Rom 3:26; Eph 2:8-9). A social hierarchy is ordained by God (see *honor*, below) to maintain order in society and the church (Rom 13:1-7; 1 Pet 5:5); hence, we are not equal in social status. However, Christians are expected to consider the needs of others and share material goods so that there will be equality (2 Cor 8:14; Phil 2:4-7).

esthetics—Beauty is an attribute of God which he bestows on his creation (Ps 27:4; 50:2; Is 4:2; 61:3); however, it is not something to be overly valued. Beauty can be temporary and unreliable (Jas 1:11), it can be misused (Prov 31:30; Ezek 16:15). Jesus did not come as a beautiful person (Is 53:2). The Christian's beauty is to come from inward character rather than outward appearance (1 Pet 3:3-4).

excellence—God demonstrates excellence to us (Is 28:29). His people are to reflect it (Dan 5:12), seek it (1 Cor 12:31) and approve what is excellent (Phil

1:10). Also see *competence.*

faith—Faith is the basis on which our ethical behavior is motivated and formed (Hab 2:4; Rom 1:16-17; 14:23; Gal 3:23-27; Eph 2:8-10; Heb 10:36-39; Jas 2:26; 2 Pet 1:3-8). It is "the assurance of things hoped for, the conviction of things not seen" (Heb 11:1). Faith consists of both belief and trust in God, which results in a dynamic personal relationship with him (Rom 3:22-26) and power to do his will (Mt 21:22; Mk 11:22-24; Heb 11).

fidelity—Faithfulness is a key attribute of God (1 Cor 1:9; 1 Jn 1:9; Lam 3:22-23). His faithfulness is unconditional, even when his people are unfaithful (Hos 14:4; Rom 3:3-4). Fidelity is an essential aspect of Christian character (Mt 25:21; 1 Cor 4:2; 1 Tim 3:11) and a fruit of the Spirit (Gal 5:22).

forgiveness—Forgiveness is an attribute of God which the Christian is also expected to offer to others (Ps 130:3-4; Jer 31:34; Mt 6:12-15; 18:35; Mk 11:25; Lk 6:37; 17:3-4; Eph 4:32). Lack of forgiveness can cause serious problems (Ps 37:8; 2 Cor 2:5-11; Heb 12:15).

freedom—Freedom is a sign of God's presence (2 Cor 3:1). The biblical concept of freedom is always set in the context of a prior captivity or bondage (Is 61:1-3; Gal 5:1). Israel gained freedom from slavery in Egypt (Ex 12:51). Jesus Christ gives us freedom from the Law (Gal 3:23-28) and from bondage to sin and death (Rom 6:17-18). Christian freedom is a paradox. We are free in order to serve God and others (1 Cor 9:19; Gal 5:1; 1 Pet 2:16). We are also free to reject the grace of God and remain in slavery to the elemental spirits of the universe (Col 2:8). In Christ we are free to be in relationship with others, requiring us to be interdependent (1 Cor 12:14-26).

generosity—The Christian is to hold loosely to material goods and share them freely and cheerfully with people in need (Mt 19:21; Lk 12:32-34; 14:12-14; Rom 12:13; 2 Cor 9:1-9; Jas 2:15-17; 1 Jn 3:17), or even with people who selfishly demand it (Mt 5:40-42; Lk 12:18).

gentleness—Gentleness is an attribute of God in Christ (Mt 11:29; 2 Cor 10:1) and a fruit of the Spirit (Gal 5:22) which should characterize our ministry (Gal 6:1; 1 Thess 2:7).

gratitude—Gratitude for God's gift of salvation is central to Christian ethics, because it provides the motivation for ethical behavior (Rom 6:17-18; 1 Cor 4:7; 15:57-58; Heb 13:15-16; 1 Pet 4:10). Thankfulness should characterize the Christian's attitude (Eph 5:4, 20; Col 2:6-7; 3:15-17; 4:2; Phil 4:6; 1 Thes 5:18).

group approval—The Bible gives little weight to outward propriety when it is unaccompanied by the right motivation and attitude (1 Sam 16:7; Mt 23;

Lk 11:37-44; Col 2:23). However, our behavior is to be beyond reproach, especially in the company of unbelievers (2 Cor 8:21; Eph 5:15; Col 4:5-6).

happiness—Throughout the Bible joy is a mark of the individual believer and of the community of faith (Ps 4:7; 105:43; Is 35:10; 51:11; 55:12; 61:7; Mt 2:10; Lk 10:17; Acts 8:8; 13:52; 1 Pet 1:8). It is a quality, not merely an emotion, which results from a dynamic, personal relationship with God (Ps 16:11; 43:3-4; Hab 3:18), and can be lost when that relationship is severed (Ps 51:12; Jas 4:8-9). Joy can be experienced in the midst of suffering (Phil 1:17-19; 1 Thess 1:6; Jas 1:2; 1 Pet 1:6-8) and often follows sorrow (Ps 30:5; 126:6; Jn 16:20-22). It is a gift of God (Is 61:3; Jer 31:13; Lk 2:10) and a fruit of the Spirit (Gal 5:22). Happiness is never seen as an end in itself in Scripture, but as a characteristic of life lived in the kingdom of God (Mt 13:44; Rom 14:17).

health—The English word *salvation* is derived from the Latin *salus*, which means "health" and "help" and translates the Greek word *soteria*, meaning "cure," "recovery," "redemption," "remedy," "rescue" and "welfare." Physical, psychosocial and spiritual health are at the heart of the gospel. Healing is a sign of the coming of God's kingdom (Is 35:3-6; 61:1; Mt 11: 2-5; Lk 4:18-21; Rev 21:3-4). Jesus demonstrated his concern for health by his healing ministry throughout the gospels. He sent his disciples out to teach, preach and heal (Mt 10:7-8; Lk 10:9). Jesus suffered that we may be healed (Is 53:5; 1 Pet 2:24). Throughout history God has been the agent of healing (Ps 103:3; 147:3; Hos 11:3). After the death and resurrection of Jesus his healing ministry was entrusted to the church (Acts 3:3-10; 28:7-9; Jas 5:13-15).

honor—The Christian is to honor and respect all people, but special esteem is expected toward God and those in positions of authority (1 Pet 2:17; Rom 12:10; 13:1-7). That honor includes fulfilling our civic duties (Rom 13:7) and honoring our parents (Ex 20:12). Lack of honor can deter effective ministry (Mt 13:57; 1 Cor 4:10). Enigmatically, the church is told to give the greater honor to the inferior parts (1 Cor 12:24). Honor is bestowed on all people by God (Ps 8:5; Heb 2:7).

hope—Christian hope is twofold. Ultimately there is the future hope of heaven and the parousia (Rom 8:18-20; Col 1:5; Rev 21:1-4) which brings joy and expectation in the midst of suffering (Rom 5:2; 1 Pet 1:6). We also have a present hope of living in the kingdom of God and experiencing the "first fruits" of salvation (Rom 8:22-24) which include healing and power over evil (Mt 10:7-8; Lk 9:1-2), the assurance of God's love and the presence and power of the Holy Spirit (Rom 5:5; 8:26-28, 38-39; 15:13), the encouragement of the

Scriptures (Rom 15:4), the expectation of gain from our labors (1 Cor 9:8-11), and comfort in grief (1 Thess 4:13). Our hope is centered in faith based on the character of God (Heb 11:1; 1 Pet 1:3-5). Hope provides the strength to endure hardship, prevents apathy, and motivates us in ministry (Heb 6:11-20).

hospitality—Hospitality is a Christian responsibility which demonstrates the reality of our faith (Rom 12:13; Jas 2:14-26; 1 Tim 5:10). Jesus expected hospitality during his earthly ministry, and he demonstrated it in John 13. He taught the disciples to expect hospitality and gave strong warnings against those who refuse to offer it (Mt 10:11-15; Luke 10:5-12). Hospitality is to be offered to the poor, the sick, the stranger, and the outcast (Mt 25:34-40; Lk 14:12-14; 3 Jn 5-8). Christian leaders are to demonstrate hospitality (1 Tim 3:2; Tit 1:8). It is to be offered ungrudgingly (1 Pet 4:9), and it often brings unexpected rewards (Heb 13:2). The early church established hospices for travelers, and later hospitals were established for the sick in order to show hospitality.

human dignity—Human worth is derived from our creation in the image of God (Gen 1:26), our position of honor in God's economy (Ps 8:4-8; Rev 22:1-5), and his willingness to suffer and die to redeem us (Jn 3:16; Heb 2:14-16). We can claim no merit of our own in our relationship with God (Rom 3:23; Rom 7:15-25; Phil 3:7-11); however, human credentials can be useful for speaking with authority in our relationships with others (2 Cor 11; Acts 21:39-40; 23:1-5, 26-30; 1 Pet 2:13-17).

humility—True humility is a clear recognition of our status before God and relationship to one another (1 Pet 5:6; Mt 18:4; 23:10-12; Rom 12:3; Eph 4:1-3; Phil 2:3; Col 3:12-17; Jas 4:6). Jesus demonstrated humility through his incarnation and death (Mt 21:5; Jn 13:1-15; Phil 2:8). Humility is the opposite of arrogance and self-centeredness. The humble/meek will be exalted by God, but the presumptuous will be humbled (Ps 37:11; 113:5-9; Prov 15:33; 18:12; Mt 5:5; 23:12; Lk 1:52; 14:7-11; 1 Pet 5:6). Humility is not a public display of piety (Mt 6:1-6), nor self-abasement (Col 2:18-23), but a willingness to accept help when needed, to serve without expectation of reward, and to be content in all circumstances, glorifying God and not ourselves (Phil 4:10-20).

integrity—Christians are to be persons of integrity. Faith results in honest and faithful behavior (Mt 5:19-20; Acts 24:15-16; 1 Tim 1:19; 1 Pet 3:16). Personal and public behavior must be consistent, and we must not judge others by standards we do not keep ourselves (Mt 6:1; 7:5; Mk 7:14-23).

interdependence—The interdependent Christian community is the expression of the character and work of Jesus Christ in the world today (Eph 4:1-16; 5:21; 1 Cor 12; Rom 12). While each person is unique and is expected to contribute to the needs of the family and community (1 Thess 5:3-8), individualism and total independence are not virtues.

justice—The Hebrew word *sedaqa* (justice) is a legal term for righteousness, which is bestowed on the believer by God and results in godly behavior. It involves goodness and loving consideration. It is used to describe "straightness" in a physical sense, and can be considered as conformity to a set of values. Hence, in a pluralistic society, the concept of justice can differ according to the values of a person or sub-group. Justice is an attribute of God (Ps 89:14; Rom 3:5) which his people are to demonstrate (Deut 16:20; Ps 37:32-34; Amos 5:24; Mt 23:23; Heb 11:33). God's justice champions the cause of the poor, the oppressed and the disfranchised (Ps 103:6-7; Is 58:6-7; Amos; Mic 2:1-10; Zech 7:8-14; Lk 4:16-21; Jas 1:27).

love—Love is the primary value for the Christian (Mt 22:36-40; Jn 13:34-35; 1 Cor 13). God is love and apart from him we cannot love others (1 Jn 4:7-21). We love others out of gratitude for the love God shows to us in Jesus Christ. True love, as demonstrated by God, is a total abandonment of self for the benefit of another, even unto death (Jn 3:16; Phil 2:1-8; Rom 5:8).

magnanimity—Aristotle advocated magnanimity as the virtue which opposes the vices of presumption, ambition, vainglory, and on the opposite end of the spectrum, pusillanimity (small-mindedness). It includes the pursuit of excellence, and is part of the virtue of courage or fortitude. Phil 4:8 is a call to magnanimity.

mercy—The Hebrew word *hesed,* also translated "steadfast love," is God's gratuitous love which forms the origin and basis for the covenant. It is a response of love, not duty (Mt 25:31-46; Jas 1:27; 1 Jn 4:19; Eph 3:31-5:2; 1 Jn 3:17; Lk 10:25-37). Inherent in the concept of mercy is the willingness to forgive and accept forgiveness (Mt 5:7; 6:14-15). Christian mercy is to be impartial, extending to enemies (Mt 5:44), outcasts (Lk 10:30-37), and the poor (Jas 2:1-6).

nonmaleficence—The principle of nonmaleficence states the duty not to harm or injure others, or to put them at risk of harm unless there are compelling reasons to do so. The Hippocratic Oath refers to nonmaleficence as "First of all, do no harm." Harm is damage to a person's interests, whether physical, psychological or of reputation. In some ethical theories this principle is considered primary, before the duty to help others. Nonmaleficence is one aspect of love. God's intent is not to harm, but to do good (Jer 29:11; Is 11:9).

obedience—Jesus demonstrated perfect obedience (Heb 5:8; Rom 5:19; Phil 2:7). God desires the obedience of all people (Rom 15:18; Eph 1:21-23; Phil 2:10). The Christian's primary obedience is to God (Acts 5:29; 1 Pet 1:14-16), then to Christian leaders (1 Pet 5:5), to one another (Eph 5:21), to parents (Ex 20:12; Eph 6:1-3), to spouses (Eph 5:22-33), to earthly masters (Eph 6:5-8), and to the governing authorities (Rom 13:1). When loyalties conflict, the Christian conscience is informed by the Scriptures (2 Tim 3:16) and the Holy Spirit (Jn 16:13; Lk 12:11-12).

old age—Throughout the Bible the elderly are honored and respected (1 Pet 5:5; Lev 19:32). God often singled out older people to provide leadership and counsel in crucial times. Abraham was 75 years old when God called him to leave his country and go to the Promised Land (Gen 12:1-4). Moses was 80 when he led Israel out of Egypt (Deut 34:7—he died at 120 after wandering in the wilderness for forty years). Simeon and Anna, two elderly people, were among the first to recognize Jesus as the Christ. Paul refered to his authority as an old man (Philem 9). The elderly are valued for their superior wisdom (Job 12:12; 15:10; 32:6-7; 1 Kings 12:6-8; Ps 119:100). They are able to teach from their experience (Titus 2:2; 1 Pet 5:1-5; 1 Jn 1:1-4). Communities with older citizens were considered greatly blessed (Is 65:20; Zech 8:4). Senior citizens are a source of tradition, order and "roots" (Ezra 3:10-12), they are a source of spiritual encouragement (Ps 37:25), and important participants in the kingdom of God (Joel 2:28). Old age is a sign of divine favor (Gen 15:14-15), a reward for piety (Ex 20:12); it brings a new kind of beauty (Prov 20:29), and is anticipated in faith and hope (Ps 71:17-21). God cares for the elderly (Is 46:4).

patience—Patience is a fruit of the Spirit (Gal 5:22) which characterizes a life of faith (Rom 8:25; Heb 6:12-15). It is also translated "endurance," "longsuffering" or "forbearance," and indicates a restraint in the midst of opposition or oppression (2 Cor 6:4; 12:12; Col 1:11). It is not passivity. It characterizes God's dealings with his sinful people (Is 30:18; 42:14; Rom 3:25).

patriotism—While the Christian is expected to respect civil government, fulfill the obligations of citizenship (Mt 17:24-27; Mk 12:13-17; Rom 13:1-7), and enjoy the benefits of citizenship (Acts 21:39), our ultimate loyalty is to the kingdom of God and the household of faith (Mt 6:33; Acts 1:6-9; Eph 2:19;

Heb 11:14-16; Rev 21:1-4).

peace—The biblical concept of peace *(shalom)* goes far beyond the absence of conflict. It means a total well-being, completeness or wholeness within the person and in interpersonal relationships. It implies the total welfare of a person or community, including material prosperity, physical safety, and spiritual well-being. Jesus is the Prince of Peace (Is 9:6) and our peace with God (Rom 5:1; Eph 2:14). Peace is an attribute of God (1 Cor 14:33) and a gift of God (Ps 26:3; Lk 2:14; Jn 14:27) which the Christian is to offer to others (Lk 10:5; Acts 10:36; 1 Pet 3:11). Peace is the result of righteousness and truth (Ps 37:37; 85:10; Is 32:17; Rom 14:17-18) and becomes effective in our lives through faith (Ps 119:165; Rom 5:1).

poverty—God has special concern for the poor and judges those who oppress them (Job 5:11-16; Ps 12:5; 35:10; 68:5-6; 69:33; 72:12-13; 103:6-7; 109:30-31; 140:12; 146:7-9; Prov 17:5; Jer 22:1-5; Amos 4:1-3; Zech 7:8-14; Lk 4:16-21). The New Testament singles out the poor as recipients of God's special blessing (Mt 5:3; Lk 6:20; 16:19-31; Jas 2:5). It is the responsibility of God's people to care for the poor (Ps 41:1; Prov 14:21; 19:17; Lk 11:37-41; 12:32-34; 14:12-14; Acts 9:36-41; Eph 4:28; Jas 2:14-17; 1 Jn 3:16-18).

power—All power belongs to God (Mt 6:13; 26:64; 2 Cor 4:7; Rev 19:1), and comes from God (Is 40:24; Lk 1:35; Jn 1:12; 17:2; Acts 1:8; Rev 2:26). By making us in his image (Gen 1:26), God shares his power with us and gives us the choice of whether to use power responsibly (for good) or irresponsibly (for evil) (Gen 1:28; 2:16-17; Josh 24:15; Amos 5:15). The Christian's task is to use the power which God gives to glorify God and bring justice to society (Mic 6:8; Rom 12:21).

productivity—The Bible places a strong value on productivity for those who are able to work (Prov 31:10-31; Mt 25:14-28; 2 Thess 3:6-12; 1 Tim 5:11-13), but a person's worth is based on being created and redeemed by God, not on ability to produce (1 Cor 1:26-31; 12:22-26, also see *efficiency*).

progress—The view that change brings positive improvement and should be fostered is a relatively modern idea with roots in the Enlightenment. Although the Bible presents a clear picture of redemptive history (e.g., Acts 7), the superiority of the New Covenant (Heb 9) and the ultimate redemption of the whole world (Rom 8; 2 Pet 3:13), there is little sense that life on earth will radically improve over time. Instead the Bible illustrates a pattern of sin and redemption repeated over and over. Change for the sake of change is not seen as progress.

prosperity—Although the Old Testament often portrays prosperity as a reward for faith (Josh 1:7-8; Ps 1:1-3; Zech 1:17) it is also shown to be an opportunity to share with others (Lev 19:9-10; 23:22; Deut 24:19-22), a concept which is reinforced in the New Testament (Lk 18:22; Acts 2:45; Rom 15:25-27; 2 Cor 8:13-15). Failure to do so is condemned (Is 5:8-10; Amos 6:1; Lk 16:19-31). The wicked also prosper (Job 21:7-16; Jer 12:1) but they will ultimately be punished for their greed (Lk 12:13-21; Eph 5:5; Col 3:5-6). Also see *generosity.*

quality of life—Judging the quality of life is highly subjective. Only God knows the true value of a person's life (1 Sam 16:7; 1 Pet 3:4). God may have plans for a person, even when the person is in total despair and wants to die (1 Kings 19:4) or when the person's life appears to be hopeless (2 Sam 1:1-16). While true quality of life comes only through a relationship with God (Jn 10:10), God continues to love and seek after those who do not respond to him (Mt 18:10-14).

respect—Christians are to respect those in authority (Rom 13:1-7; Eph 6:5), the elderly (1 Pet 5:5), parents (Ex 20:12; Eph 6:1), spouses (Eph 5:24-30) and one another (Eph 5:21). See *honor.*

sanctity of life—All human life has value. God created human beings in his own image (Gen 1:26-27). God took on human form in Jesus Christ (Jn 1:14; Eph 2:5-7). Through his care and compassion, Jesus Christ reinforced the worth of all persons: the disabled, diseased and oppressed (see Gospel accounts). People are so valuable that Christ died for them (Jn 3:16; Rom 5:8). Life begins at conception (Jer 1:5; Gen 21:1-2; Lk 1:13; Ps 139:13-16; Job 10:8-12). Destroying life, whether through abortion or euthanasia, is diametrically opposed to God's purpose for creating life (Ex 20:13; Rom 13:9-10). [From "This We Believe About Life and Its Value," Nurses Christian Fellowship, 1980.]

security—For the Christian, security comes from a relationship with God (Ps 4:8; 46:1-2), not in earthly situations (Ps 91; Prov 29:25; Mt 23:37; 2 Cor 4:7-18, 1 Thess 5:3). Trusting in anything other than God will lead to a false sense of security (Judg 18:7-10; Jer 6:13-15).

self-actualization—The concept of self-actualization as a human accomplishment is foreign to the Bible. The ultimate goal for the Christian is to grow increasingly like Jesus Christ and to reflect his glory (2 Cor 3:18; Eph 1:5-14 and 4:15). Jesus said, "For those who want to save their life will lose it, and those who lose their life for my sake will find it" (Mt 16:25 NRSV). We are created in the image of God (Gen 1:26) and the only way to become what we were created to be is to live in subjection to the Lord Jesus Christ. In that process, many of the characteristics of "self-actualization" are realized in a person's life.

serving—Service is basic to the Christian life. Jesus said, "Whoever would be first among you must be your slave; even as the Son of man came not to be served, but to serve" (Mt 20:27-28). We are to follow his example (Phil 2:3-18; 1 Pet 2:21). We serve in a variety of ways, according to the gifts given to us by God (Rom 12; 1 Cor 12; Eph 4).

suffering—The Bible presents suffering as an enigma. It is the result of the Fall (Gen 3:14-19) and, especially in pre-exilic Israel, often seen as a sign of judgment for sin (Num 12:1-15; Deut 32:49-52; 2 Sam 12:7-18; 2 Kings 5:20-27; Job 4:7-8; 8:4; 15:20; Ps 32:3-4; 39:11; Jer 31:29-30; Ezek 18:2-4; Amos 1—2; Lk 13:1-5; Jn 9:2). But even in the Old Testament suffering was presented in a positive light for its refining properties (Job 42:1-6; Ps 137; Hab 3:16-19; Mal 3:2-3), a theme reinforced in the New Testament (Mt 5:11-12; Rom 5:3-5; 8:17; 2 Cor 12:7-10; Phil 1:29-30; Jas 5:10-11; 1 Pet 1:6-7). Suffering is sent by Satan, but allowed by God (Job 2:6; 2 Cor 12:7). Jesus suffered the penalty for our sin so that we can be redeemed from sin and death (Mk 8:31; Lk 24:45-47; Rom 5:6-8). Jesus initiated the kingdom of God on earth by relieving human suffering and sending others out to do the same (Mt 11:4-5; Mk 6:13; Lk 9:2). The relief of some suffering is a "first fruit" of the kingdom (Rom 8:18-25) where there will ultimately be no suffering at all (1 Pet 5:10; Rev 21:2-4). God expects Christians to work toward relieving human suffering (Is 58:6-7; Mt 25:34-40; Jn 14:12; 2 Thess 3:13; 1 Tim 5:10; Jas 2:14-16; 5:13-15; 1 Jn 3:17-18), but we are not to be surprised by suffering, and can rejoice that through our suffering we share in the suffering of Christ (1 Pet 4:12-13; Phil 3:8-11).

technology—The ability of people to invent tools to accomplish work is a reflection of our being created in the image of God (Gen 1:26). Technology in itself is neutral, but it can be used for either good or evil. We are not to put our trust in technology (Is 31:1; Ps 20:7-8) or to worship the work of our hands (Is 44:9-20). It is not to be used presumptuously to declare our independence from God (Gen 11:1-8). Modern technology, while alleviating some forms of suffering and improving standards of living from a material perspective, has raised new ethical and moral issues, such as environmental concerns, allocation of scarce resources, control of human reproduction and genetics, and termination of life.

temperance—Temperance (also translated "self-control") is primarily seen as a fruit of the Spirit in the New Testament (Gal 5:23; 2 Tim 1:7). It is a desired Christian virtue which makes ministry more effective (2 Pet 1:6; 1 Tim 3:11; 1 Cor 9:25-27; Tit 2:2).

tolerance—The Bible draws a fine line between being nonjudgmental and being discerning. We are not to be hypocritical, judging others when we are equally guilty of sin (Mt 7:1; Jn 8:7; Rom 14:13); on the other hand, sin in the church is to be recognized and dealt with firmly (Lk 17:3; Rom 16:17; Gal 5:12; 1 Cor 1:11; 5:1-13; 2 Cor 12:20-21; 13:2-3; Gal 3:1-3; Eph 5:11; Phil 4:2; 2 Thess 3:14-15), but gently (2 Cor 10:1; Gal 6:1). Judgment is ultimately reserved for God (1 Cor 4:3-5; Jas 4:11-12), especially for those outside the church (1 Cor 5:12-13). See chapter two for a more detailed treatment of judging others.

tradition—The importance of tradition has held a firm place in the Bible and church history (2 Thess 2:15; 3:6; 1 Cor 11:2), but not all traditions hold equal weight. Traditions which are not of God are condemned (Mt 15:2; Mk 7:5-8; Col 2:8). Tradition can provide order and stability in a person's life, but it must not be so rigidly followed that we cannot allow for change when necessary.

truth—The biblical concept of truth has several dimensions. In its simplest form it is an intellectual validation of facts (Deut 17:4; 1 Kings 10:6-7), but more commonly it refers to a character trait of faithfulness, dependability and reliability (Gen 42:16; Ps 51:6; Is 59:14-15; Jn 4:24), which is an attribute of God (Jer 10:10; Ps 43:3; Jn 1:14; Rom 3:3-8). Jesus identified himself as the Truth (Jn 14:6), the Holy Spirit as the Spirit of truth (Jn 14:17), and God's Word as truth (Jn 17:17). The Christian's responsibility for truth includes guarding it (2 Tim 1:14), receiving knowledge about it (Heb 10:26), obeying it (1 Pet 1:22) and being established in it (2 Pet 1:12). We must be "of the truth" to hear the voice of Jesus (Jn 18:37) and speak the truth to one another (Eph 4:25).

vengeance—Revenge is reserved for God alone in the Bible (Deut 32:35-36; Rom 12:17-21). Jesus instructed his followers to love their enemies and pray for those who persecute them (Mt 5:38-48; Lk 6:27-36), a principle followed in the early church (Rom 12:14; 1 Pet 3:9). Among believers even a lawsuit should be unnecessary (1 Cor 6:1-8).

wisdom—True wisdom is an attribute of God demonstrated to the world through Jesus Christ (Lk 2:40, 52; Mt 11:19; 12:42; 13:54; Mk 6:2; Rev 5:12). Wisdom is a gift from God which can be requested (1 Kings 4:29; Jas 1:5). Godly wisdom is pure, peaceable, gentle, open to reason, full of mercy and good fruits, without uncertainty or insincerity; it leads to righteousness and peace (Jas 3:17-18). Worldly wisdom is inferior, often contrary to God's will, and can be disastrous (Is 5:21; 19:11; Jer 18:18; Ezek 28:1-10; Rom 1:22; 1 Cor 1:17-25; Jas 3:13-16). Prudence, a wisdom which involves a reasoned judgment about the means to achieve an end, is advocated by Jesus (Mt 7:24-27; 10:16; 25:1-30; Lk 14:28-32; 16:1-9).

youth—In the Bible youth is a time for humility (Jer 1:6), learning and growth (Deut 6:7; Prov 22:6; Ps 71:17; Lk 2:40, 46; 2 Tim 3:14-15), and making mistakes (Ps 25:7; Is 54:4). Yet at times God appoints those in their youth to leadership positions and in such cases they should be respected (1 Sam 3; 1 Tim 4:12).

zeal—Zeal is a fervent commitment to a cause. The zeal of God will establish his kingdom (Is 9:7), as demonstrated by Jesus in Jn 2:13-17. Zeal should characterize our discipleship (Rom 12:8-11; 1 Pet 3:13; 2 Pet 1:10; 3:14), and can be an encouragement to other Christians (2 Cor 9:2). Zeal can also be misdirected (Lk 6:15; Rom 10:2; Phil 3:6).

APPENDIX B:
SURVEY OF NURSING VALUES

1. Questionnaire

2. Survey Results

Demographics
Table I—Major Sources of Stress in Clinical Practice
Table II—Motivation to Continue Working in Stressful
    Environment
Table III—Ideal Personal Characteristics of the Nurse
Table IV—Comparative Rating of Values
Table V—Values Rated Extremely Important

Survey of Nursing Values

PLEASE MARK THE APPROPRIATE BOXES WITH AN "X":
(Fill in blanks when appropriate.)

1. Status: RN □ A   LPN/LVN □ B   Student □ C (Grad. Date_____)

2. Education: Diploma   □ A   **3.** State of Residence: _____
                   Assoc. Degree □ B   **4.** Age: _____
                   Baccalaureate □ C   **5.** Sex: M   F
                   Master's   □ D   **6.** Marital Status: S M W D
                   Doctorate   □ E   **7.** Number of Years in Nursing: _____

8. Place of   Hospital   □ A   School of Nursing   □ F
   Employment: Nursing Home   □ B   Community Health
                                                           Agency   □ G
                      Private Duty   □ C   School   □ H
                      Temp. Agency   □ D   Industry   □ I
                      Private Prac.   □ E   Other _____ □ J
          For-Profit Agency □ Y   Non-Profit Agency □ Z

9. Area of   Comm. Health □ A   OB/Newborn   □ G
Nursing Practice: Critical Care   □ B   Oncology   □ H
(primary focus)   Geriatrics   □ C   OR/Anesthesia   □ I
                          Hospice   □ D   Pediatrics   □ J
                          Med/Surg   □ E   Rehab   □ K
                          Mental Health □ F   Other _____ □ L

10. Position: Director of Nursing □ A   Nurse Practitioner   □ F
                        Supervisor or Asst. □ B   Administrator or Asst. □ G
                        Head Nurse or Asst. □ C   Inservice Educator   □ H
                        Staff Nurse   □ D   Faculty Member   □ I
                        Clinical Specialist □ E   Other _____ □ J

11. Ethnic origin:

Asian □ A   Black □ B   Caucasian □ C   Hispanic □ H   Other □ O

12. Religion: _____

13. How important are your religious beliefs to you?

Extremely □ A Very □ B Somewhat □ C Minimal □ D Not at all □ E

14. What are the three (3) most significant reasons you chose nursing as a career?

Salary and benefits	□ A	Job security/availability	□ G
To help other people	□ B	To serve God	□ H
Role model of nurses I admired	□ C	Aptitude and ability	□ I
Parental pressure	□ D	Affordable education	□ J
Compassion for the sick	□ E	Liked the uniform	□ K
Preparation for other goals	□ F	Other _____	□ L

15. How satisfied do you feel with nursing as a career?

I love it	□ A	Somewhat dissatisfied	□ O
Usually happy in it	□ B	Hate it, but sticking with it	□ E
Somewhat satisfied	□ C	Ready to quit or have quit	□ F

16. What is your usual response to conflict?

Avoid it □ A Stay neutral □ B Facilitate □ C Take sides □ O

17. What are the problems you most often face in nursing which create stress for you?

18. What motivates you to perform your work in such difficult situations?

19. What personal characteristics do you think nurses should have in order to provide good nursing care?

1 = Extremely important   4 = Relatively unimportant
2 = Mildly important   5 = Strongly reject
3 = Neutral

20. Please circle the number of importance you attach to each of the following values using the scale provided:

1	2	3	4	5	altruism	1	2	3	4	5	hope
1	2	3	4	5	ambition	1	2	3	4	5	human dignity
1	2	3	4	5	assertiveness	1	2	3	4	5	humility
1	2	3	4	5	authority	1	2	3	4	5	integrity
1	2	3	4	5	autonomy	1	2	3	4	5	interdependence
1	2	3	4	5	beneficence	1	2	3	4	5	justice
1	2	3	4	5	compassion	1	2	3	4	5	love
1	2	3	4	5	competence	1	2	3	4	5	patience
1	2	3	4	5	confidentiality	1	2	3	4	5	peace
1	2	3	4	5	cost-effectiveness	1	2	3	4	5	power
1	2	3	4	5	courage	1	2	3	4	5	productivity
1	2	3	4	5	duty	1	2	3	4	5	progress
1	2	3	4	5	education	1	2	3	4	5	prosperity
1	2	3	4	5	efficiency	1	2	3	4	5	quality of life
1	2	3	4	5	encouragement	1	2	3	4	5	respect
1	2	3	4	5	equality	1	2	3	4	5	sanctity of life
1	2	3	4	5	esthetics	1	2	3	4	5	security
1	2	3	4	5	excellence	1	2	3	4	5	self-actualization
1	2	3	4	5	faith	1	2	3	4	5	serving
1	2	3	4	5	fidelity	1	2	3	4	5	technology
1	2	3	4	5	forgiveness	1	2	3	4	5	tolerance
1	2	3	4	5	freedom	1	2	3	4	5	tradition
1	2	3	4	5	group approval	1	2	3	4	5	truth
1	2	3	4	5	happiness	1	2	3	4	5	vengeance
1	2	3	4	5	health	1	2	3	4	5	wisdom

1 = Extremely important   4 = Relatively unimportant
2 = Mildly important   5 = Strongly reject
3 = Neutral

21. Rate the importance of each of the following values in governing nursing practice in your work setting:

1	2	3	4	5	altruism	1	2	3	4	5	hope
1	2	3	4	5	ambition	1	2	3	4	5	human dignity
1	2	3	4	5	assertiveness	1	2	3	4	5	humility
1	2	3	4	5	authority	1	2	3	4	5	integrity
1	2	3	4	5	autonomy	1	2	3	4	5	interdependence
1	2	3	4	5	beneficence	1	2	3	4	5	justice
1	2	3	4	5	compassion	1	2	3	4	5	love
1	2	3	4	5	competence	1	2	3	4	5	patience
1	2	3	4	5	confidentiality	1	2	3	4	5	peace
1	2	3	4	5	cost-effectiveness	1	2	3	4	5	power
1	2	3	4	5	courage	1	2	3	4	5	productivity
1	2	3	4	5	duty	1	2	3	4	5	progress
1	2	3	4	5	education	1	2	3	4	5	prosperity
1	2	3	4	5	efficiency	1	2	3	4	5	quality of life
1	2	3	4	5	encouragement	1	2	3	4	5	respect
1	2	3	4	5	equality	1	2	3	4	5	sanctity of life
1	2	3	4	5	esthetics	1	2	3	4	5	security
1	2	3	4	5	excellence	1	2	3	4	5	self-actualization
1	2	3	4	5	faith	1	2	3	4	5	serving
1	2	3	4	5	fidelity	1	2	3	4	5	technology
1	2	3	4	5	forgiveness	1	2	3	4	5	tolerance
1	2	3	4	5	freedom	1	2	3	4	5	tradition
1	2	3	4	5	group approval	1	2	3	4	5	truth
1	2	3	4	5	happiness	1	2	3	4	5	vengeance
1	2	3	4	5	health	1	2	3	4	5	wisdom

1 = Extremely important   4 = Relatively unimportant
2 = Mildly important   5 = Strongly reject
3 = Neutral

22. Rate the importance of each of the following values as correctives to problems in your work setting:

1 2 3 4 5		1 2 3 4 5	
1 2 3 4 5	altruism	1 2 3 4 5	hope
1 2 3 4 5	ambition	1 2 3 4 5	human dignity
1 2 3 4 5	assertiveness	1 2 3 4 5	humility
1 2 3 4 5	authority	1 2 3 4 5	integrity
1 2 3 4 5	autonomy	1 2 3 4 5	interdependence
1 2 3 4 5	beneficence	1 2 3 4 5	justice
1 2 3 4 5	compassion	1 2 3 4 5	love
1 2 3 4 5	competence	1 2 3 4 5	patience
1 2 3 4 5	confidentiality	1 2 3 4 5	peace
1 2 3 4 5	cost-effectiveness	1 2 3 4 5	power
1 2 3 4 5	courage	1 2 3 4 5	productivity
1 2 3 4 5	duty	1 2 3 4 5	progress
1 2 3 4 5	education	1 2 3 4 5	prosperity
1 2 3 4 5	efficiency	1 2 3 4 5	quality of life
1 2 3 4 5	encouragement	1 2 3 4 5	respect
1 2 3 4 5	equality	1 2 3 4 5	sanctity of life
1 2 3 4 5	esthetics	1 2 3 4 5	security
1 2 3 4 5	excellence	1 2 3 4 5	self-actualization
1 2 3 4 5	faith	1 2 3 4 5	serving
1 2 3 4 5	fidelity	1 2 3 4 5	technology
1 2 3 4 5	forgiveness	1 2 3 4 5	tolerance
1 2 3 4 5	freedom	1 2 3 4 5	tradition
1 2 3 4 5	group approval	1 2 3 4 5	truth
1 2 3 4 5	happiness	1 2 3 4 5	vengeance
1 2 3 4 5	health	1 2 3 4 5	wisdom

1 = Extremely important   4 = Relatively unimportant
2 = Mildly important   5 = Strongly reject
3 = Neutral

23. On the following list rate the compatibility each value has with your religious beliefs:

1	2	3	4	5	altruism	1	2	3	4	5	hope
1	2	3	4	5	ambition	1	2	3	4	5	human dignity
1	2	3	4	5	assertiveness	1	2	3	4	5	humility
1	2	3	4	5	authority	1	2	3	4	5	integrity
1	2	3	4	5	autonomy	1	2	3	4	5	interdependence
1	2	3	4	5	beneficence	1	2	3	4	5	justice
1	2	3	4	5	compassion	1	2	3	4	5	love
1	2	3	4	5	competence	1	2	3	4	5	patience
1	2	3	4	5	confidentiality	1	2	3	4	5	peace
1	2	3	4	5	cost-effectiveness	1	2	3	4	5	power
1	2	3	4	5	courage	1	2	3	4	5	productivity
1	2	3	4	5	duty	1	2	3	4	5	progress
1	2	3	4	5	education	1	2	3	4	5	prosperity
1	2	3	4	5	efficiency	1	2	3	4	5	quality of life
1	2	3	4	5	encouragement	1	2	3	4	5	respect
1	2	3	4	5	equality	1	2	3	4	5	sanctity of life
1	2	3	4	5	esthetics	1	2	3	4	5	security
1	2	3	4	5	excellence	1	2	3	4	5	self-actualization
1	2	3	4	5	faith	1	2	3	4	5	serving
1	2	3	4	5	fidelity	1	2	3	4	5	technology
1	2	3	4	5	forgiveness	1	2	3	4	5	tolerance
1	2	3	4	5	freedom	1	2	3	4	5	tradition
1	2	3	4	5	group approval	1	2	3	4	5	truth
1	2	3	4	5	happiness	1	2	3	4	5	vengeance
1	2	3	4	5	health	1	2	3	4	5	wisdom

Results of NCF Survey of Nursing Values

Sample consisted of 1500 questionnaires sent to randomly selected subscribers to the *Journal of Christian Nursing*. Total questionnaires returned was 354.

1. Status

RN = 89%   LPN/LVN = 6%   Student = 4%

2. Education

Diploma = 24%
Associate = 20%
Baccalaureate = 35%
Master's = 15%
Doctorate = 3%

3. State of Residence

Forty-six states represented. States with greatest representation were (number responding):

Calif. = 29		Penn. = 19	
Ill. = 25		N.Y. = 17	
Ohio = 25		Wis. = 13	
Mich. = 20		Oreg. = 11	
Tex. = 20		Wash. = 10	

4. Age

Ages ranged from 22 to 69. Seventy-one per cent were 47 or younger, with a fairly even spread between 22 and 47.

5. Sex

M = 2%   F = 96%   (2% left item blank)

6. Marital Status

S = 25%   M = 64%   W = 2%   D = 7%

7. Number of Years in Nursing

Ranged from 0-46 years. Fifty per cent had worked less than 12 years, 75% less than 23 years.

8. Place of Employment

Hospital = 60%	School of Nursing = 11%
Nursing home = 9%	Comm. Health Agency = 6%
Private duty = 1%	School = 1%
Temp. agency = 1%	Industry = less than 1%
Private prac. = 2%	Other = 8%

9. Area of Nursing Practice

Comm. health = 9%	OB/newborn = 7%
Critical care = 12%	Oncology = 4%
Geriatrics = 13%	OR/anesthesia = 3%
Hospice = 2%	Pediatrics = 5%
Med./surg. = 21%	Rehab. = 2%
Mental health = 4%	Other = 19%

10. Position

Director of nursing = 3%	Nurse practitioner = 1%
Supervisor or asst. = 7%	Adminstrator or asst. = 2%
Head nurse or asst. = 10%	In-service educator = less than 1%
Staff nurse = 55%	Faculty member = 8%
Clinical specialist = 4%	Other = 9%

11. Ethnic Origin

Asian = 1%   Black = 2%   Caucasian = 94%   Hispanic = 1%   Other = 1%

12. Religion

100% were Christian

13. Importance of religious beliefs to respondent

Extremely = 82%   Very = 16%   Somewhat = 1%

14. Most significant reasons for choosing nursing

Help other people = 82%
Compassion for sick = 42%
Aptitude and abil. = 23%
Afford. educ. = 12%
Other goals = 7%
Other = 5%

Serve God = 55%
Job security/avail. = 35%
Role model of nurses = 13%
Salary and benefits = 7%
Parental pressure = 5%
Liked uniform = 1%

15. Satisfaction with nursing

Love it = 31%
Usually happy = 45%
Somewhat satisfied = 13%

Somewhat dissatisfied = 7%
Hate it, but staying = 3%
Quit/quitting = 1%

16. Usual response to conflict

Avoid it = 24%   Stay neutral = 1%   Facilitate = 43%   Take sides = 6%

17.-19. Results and source

Results summarized in tables I—III. These questions were adapted with permission from a research project by Susie Kim, RN, DNSc., Dean, College of Nursing, Ewha Women's University, Seoul, Korea.

20.-23. Results summarized in tables IV and V.

Table I

Major Sources of Stress in Clinical Practice among Nurses in the United States

n = 354

Source of stress	frequency	percentage
1. Interpersonal conflicts	187	53%
(with other nurses)	(88)	(25%)
(with physicians)	(41)	(12%)
(with other departments)	(10)	(3%)
(with patients' families)	(9)	(3%)
(with patients)	(5)	(1%)
(with management)	(5)	(1%)
(nonspecific)	(29)	(8%)
2. Work overload	155	44%
3. Frustration with administration	56	16%
4. Feelings of inadequacy	33	9%
5. Ethical issues	28	8%
6. Paperwork	22	6%
7. Agency/institution budget	18	5%
8. Professional concerns	16	5%
9. Lack of respect	16	5%
10. High risk	14	4%
11. Inadequate pay	12	3%
12. Death and dying	9	3%

Table II

Motivation to Continue Working in Stressful Environment among U.S. Nurses

n = 352

Source of motivation	frequency	percentage
1. Want to help people	182	52%
2. Want to serve God	131	37%
3. Enjoy nursing	65	18%
4. Support of coworkers	27	8%
5. Need the money	21	6%
6. Take one day at a time	14	4%
7. Commitment to nursing	11	2%
8. Despair/no motivation	8	2%
9. Faith/hope for change	7	2%
10. Flexible hours	5	1%
11. Role model for younger nurses	4	1%

Table III

Personal Characteristics of Nurse

n = 354

Characteristic	frequency	percentage
1. Compassionate/caring/loving	350	99%
2. Patience/endurance	104	29%
3. Competence	97	27%
4. Faith in God	88	25%
5. Honesty/integrity	85	24%
6. Kindness	60	17%
7. Self-confidence	54	15%
8. Good listener/understanding	50	14%
9. Team player	48	14%
10. Organizational skills	46	13%
11. Sense of humor	39	11%
12. Tolerant/nonjudgmental	35	10%
13. Dedication	37	10%
14. Willing to learn	29	8%
15. Assertive	28	8%

Table IV

Comparative Rating of Values

P = personal value   W = work value
C = corrective value   R = religious value

Important (–)   Extremely Important (+)

```
                30%   40%   50%   60%   70%   80%   90%  100%      %
compassion    P---------------------------------------------+++   92/98
              W------------------------+++++++++++++++           65/87
              C------------------------+++++++++++++++           67/89
              R--------------------------------------------++    94/98

competence    P--------------------------------------------++    94/97
              W--------------------------------+++++++++++       80/95
              C--------------------------------+++++++++++++     74/92
              R----------------------+++++++++++++++++++++++++   63/97

confidentiality P-----------------------------------------+++++  90/97
              W------------------------------+++++++++++++       73/91
              C----------------------------+++++++++           71/84
              R----------------------------+++++++++++++++      79/97

efficiency    P-------------------++++++++++++++++++++++++++++   57/94
              W---------------------++++++++++++++++++++++++     63/91
              C------------------++++++++++++++++++++++++        56/85
              R---------------+++++++++++++++++++++++++++++++    46/94

encouragement P-------------------------------++++++++++++++    78/96
              W--------------------++++++++++++++++++            55/80
              C------------------------------+++++++++++++      75/92
              R-----------------------------------+++++++       86/96

faith         P-----------------------------------------+++++  90/97
              W----------------++++++++++++++                   52/71
              C------------------------------+++++++++++++++    67/83
              R-------------------------------------------+    96/97

fidelity      P-------------------------------++++++++++++++    75/94
              W---------------++++++++++++++++                  52/71
              C-----------------------------+++++++++++++       67/83
              R-----------------------------------------+++++  89/94
```

Table IV (continued)

Comparative Rating of Values

P = personal value   W = work value
C = corrective value   R = religious value

Important (–)   Extremely Important (+)

	30%	40%	50%	60%	70%	80%	90%	100%	%
forgiveness	P————————————————————————+++++++++++								82/97
	W———————————++++++++++++++								51/71
	C————————————————————+++++++++++								70/85
	R——————————————————————————————+								96/97
hope	P——————————————————————————+++++++								84/97
	W——————————————+++++++++++++++								56/80
	C———————————————————+++++++++++++++++								64/87
	R————————————————————————————+++								94/97
human dignity	P——————————————————————————+++++++								87/97
	W——————————————————+++++++++++++++++++								69/92
	C———————————————————————+++++++								73/81
	R———————————————————————————+++								91/97
integrity	P——————————————————————————+++++								89/97
	W———————————————————++++++++++++++++++								66/88
	C——————————————————————+++++++++++++								76/91
	R————————————————————————————++++								90/97
love	P——————————————————————————++++++								88/97
	W——————————————+++++++++++++++++								54/75
	C———————————————————————+++++++++++++								70/87
	R—————————————————————————————++								95/97
patience	P—————————————————————————+++++++++								81/97
	W—————————————————++++++++++++++++++								57/81
	C———————————————————————+++++++++++++								76/91
	R————————————————————————————+++								93/97
productivity	P————+++++++++++++++++++++++++++++++++++								35/85
	W———————————————————+++++++++++++++++++++								55/90
	C——————————+++++++++++++++++++++++++++++++								45/85
	R———++++++++++++++++++++++++++++++++++++++								36/85

Table IV (continued)

Comparative Rating of Values

P = personal value   W = work value
C = corrective value   R = religious value

Important (–)   Extremely Important (+)

	30% 40% 50% 60% 70% 80% 90% 100%	%
quality of life	P——————————————————++++++++++++++++++	71/93
	W ————————————————++++++++++++++++	61/86
	C ——————————————-+++++++++++++++++	64/86
	R ——————————————————++++++++++++++++	70/93
respect	P—————————————————————+++++++++++++	78/97
	W ————————————————————+++++++++++++++++	67/88
	C —————————————————————++++++++++++	77/94
	R ———————————————————————————+++++++	86/97
life	P—————————————————————————+++++++	84/97
	W —————————————————————++++++++++++++	65/86
	C ——————————————————-+++++++++++	69/83
	R ——————————————————————————————+++++	90/97
serving	P——————————————+++++++++++++++++++++++++++++	57/89
	W ——————————++++++++++++++++++++++	49/80
	C ——————————————-+++++++++++++++++++++++	56/84
	R ——————————————————————————————++	87/89
tolerance	P——————————————-++++++++++++++++++++++++++++++	49/89
	W ——————————-+++++++++++++++++++++	45/76
	C ——————————————————++++++++++++++++++	58/87
	R ————————————————————++	62/64
truth	P——————————————————————————————+++++++	89/98
	W ———————————————————————+++++++++++++++++	65/88
	C ————————————————————————+++++++++++++	75/91
	R ——————————————————————————————————+++	94/98
wisdom	P——————————————————————+++++++++++++++++	70/94
	W —————————————————++++++++++++++++++++++	52/82
	C ————————————————————————+++++++++++++++++	68/90
	R ———————————————————————————————+++++	85/94

Table V

Values Rated Extremely Important

Compilation of Top Ten in Each Category

P = personal   W = work   C = corrective   R = religious

* = top ten in category

	50% 60% 70% 80% 90% 100%
compassion	P +++ 92*
	W +++++++++++++++ 65*
	C ++++++++++++++++ 67
	R ++ 94*
competence	P +++ +++ 94*
	W ++++++++++++++++++++++++++++++++++ 80*
	C +++++++++++++++++++++++++++ 74*
	R ++++++++++++++++ 63
confidentiality	P ++ 88*
	W ++++++++++++++++++++++++++ 73*
	C +++++++++++++++++++++++++ 71*
	R +++++++++++++++++++++++++++++++ 79
efficiency	P +++++++ 56
	W ++++++++++++++ 63*
	C +++++++ 56
	R 46
encouragement	P +++++++++++++++++++++++++++++++ 78
	W +++ 54
	C ++++++++++++++++++++++++++++ 75*
	R ++ 86*
faith	P ++ 89*
	W +++ 52
	C ++++++++++++++++++++++++++++ 67
	R +++ 96*

Table V (continued)

Values Rated Extremely Important

Compilation of Top Ten in Each Category

P = personal   W = work   C = corrective   R = religious
* = top ten in category

	50%	60%	70%	80%	90%	100%

encouragement P ++++++++++++++++++++++++++++++++ 78
W ++++ 54
C +++++++++++++++++++++++++++++ 75*
R +++ 86*

faith P +++ 89*
W +++ 52
C +++++++++++++++++ 67
R +++ 96*

forgiveness P ++++++++++++++++++++++++++++++++++++ 82
W +++ 51
C ++++++++++++++++++ 69*
R ++ 95*

hope P ++ 84*
W ++++++ 56
C +++++++++++++++++ 64*
R +++ 94*

human dignity P ++ 88*
W +++++++++++++++++++++ 69*
C ++++++++++++++++++++++++++++ 73*
R +++ 91*

integrity P ++ 88*
W +++++++++++++++++++ 66*
C +++++++++++++++++++++++++++ 76*
R ++ 90*

Table V (continued)

Values Rated Extremely Important

Compilation of Top Ten in Each Category

P = personal   W = work   C = corrective   R = religious

* = top ten in category

	50%	60%	70%	80%	90%	100%

love
P ++ 88*
W ++++ 54
C +++++++++++++++++++++++ 70*
R ++ 95*

patience
P +++++++++++++++++++++++++++++++++++++ 81
W +++++++ 57
C +++++++++++++++++++++++++++++ 76*
R +++ 93*

quality of life
P +++++++++++++++++++++++ 71
W +++++++++++++ 61*
C +++++++++++++++++ 64
R ++++++++++++++++++++++ 70

respect
P ++++++++++++++++++++++++++++++++++ 78
W ++++++++++++++++++ 67*
C +++++++++++++++++++++++++++++++ 77*
R +++ 86

sanctity of life
P ++ 84*
W +++++++++++++++++ 65*
C ++++++++++++++++++++++++ 69
R ++ 90*

truth
P +++ 89*
W +++++++++++++++++ 65*
C ++++++++++++++++++++++++++++++ 75*
R ++ 94*

APPENDIX C:
CODE FOR NURSES
with Interpretive Statements

Published by American Nurses' Association
2420 Pershing Road
Kansas City, Missouri 64108

G-56 12M 7/85

PREAMBLE

A code of ethics makes explicit the primary goals and values of the profession. When individuals become nurses, they make a moral commitment to uphold the values and special moral obligations expressed in their code. The Code for Nurses is based on a belief about the nature of individuals, nursing, health, and society. Nursing encompasses the protection, promotion, and restoration of health: the prevention of illness; and the alleviation of suffering in the care of clients, including individuals, families, groups, and communities. In the context of these functions, nursing is defined as the diagnosis and treatment of human responses to actual or potential health problems.

Since clients themselves are the primary decision makers in matters concerning their own health, treatment, and well-being, the goal of nursing actions is to support and enhance the client's responsibility and self-determination in the greatest extent possible. In this context, health is not necessarily an end in itself, but rather a means to a life that is meaningful from the client's perspective.

When making clinical judgments, nurses base their decisions on consideration of consequences and of universal moral principles, both of which prescribe and justify nursing actions. The most fundamental of these principles is respect for persons. Other principles stemming from this basic principle are autonomy (self-determination), beneficence (doing good), nonmaleficence (avoiding harm), veracity (truth-telling), confidentiality (respecting privileged information), fidelity (keeping promises), and justice (treating people fairly).

In brief, then, the statements of the code and their interpretation provide guidance for conduct and relationships in carrying out nursing responsibilities consistent with the ethical obligations of the profession and with high quality in nursing care.

Introduction

A code of ethics indicates a profession's acceptance of the responsibility and trust with which it has been invested by society. Under the terms of the implicit contract between society and the nursing profession, society grants the profession considerable autonomy and authority to function in the conduct of its affairs. The development of a code of ethics is an essential activity of a profession and provides one means for the exercise of professional self-regulation.

Upon entering the profession, each nurse inherits a measure of both the responsibility and the trust that have accrued to nursing over the years, as well as the corresponding obligation to adhere to the profession's code of conduct and relationships for ethical practice. The Code for Nurses with Interpretive Statements is thus more a collective expression of nursing conscience and philosophy than a set of external rules imposed upon an individual practitioner of nursing. Personal and professional integrity can be assured only if an individual is committed to the profession's code of conduct.

A code of ethical conduct offers general principles to guide and evaluate nursing actions. It does not assure the virtues required for professional practice within the character of each nurse. In particular situations, the justification of behavior as ethical must satisfy not only the individual nurse acting as a moral agent but also the standards for professional peer review.

The Code for Nurses was adopted by the American Nurses' Association in 1950 and has been revised periodically. It serves to inform both the nurse and society of the profession's expectations and requirements in ethical matters. The code and the interpretive statements together provide a framework within which nurses can make ethical decisions and discharge their responsibilities to the public, to other members of the health team, and to the profession.

Although a particular situation by its nature may determine the use of specific moral principles, the basic philosophical values, directives, and suggestions provided here are widely applicable to situations encountered in clinical practice. The Code for Nurses is not open to negotiation in employment settings, nor is it permissible for individuals or groups of nurses to adapt or change the language of this code.

The requirements of the code may often exceed those of the law. Violations of the law may subject the nurse to civil or criminal liability. The state nurses' associations, in fulfilling the profession's duty to society, may discipline their members for violations of the code. Loss of the respect and confidence of society and of one's colleagues is a serious sanction resulting from violation of the code. In addition, every nurse has a personal obligation to uphold and adhere to the code and to ensure that nursing colleagues do likewise.

Guidance and assistance in applying the code to local situations may be obtained from the American Nurses' Association and the constituent state nurses' associations.

Code for Nurses

1 The nurse provides services with respect for human dignity and the uniqueness of the client, unrestricted by considerations of social or economic status, personal attributes, or the nature of health problems.

2 The nurse safeguards the client's right to privacy by judiciously protecting information of a confidential nature.

3 The nurse acts to safeguard the client and the public when health care and safety are affected by the incompetent, unethical, or illegal practice of any person.

4 The nurse assumes responsibility and accountability. for individual nursing judgments and actions.

5 The nurse maintains competence in nursing.

6 The nurse exercises informed judgment and uses individual competence and qualifications as criteria in seeking consultation, accepting responsibilities and delegating nursing activities to others.

7 The nurse participates in activities that contribute to the ongoing development of the profession's body of knowledge.

8 The nurse participates in the profession's efforts to implement and improve standards of nursing.

9 The nurse participates in the profession's efforts to establish and maintain conditions of employment conducive to high quality nursing care.
10 The nurse participates in the profession's effort to protect the public from misinformation and misrepresentation and to maintain the integrity of nursing.
11 The nurse collaborates with members of the health professions and other citizens in promoting community and national efforts to meet the health needs of the public.

Code for Nurses with Interpretive Statements
1 The nurse provides services with respect for human dignity and the uniqueness of the client, unrestricted by considerations of social or economic status, personal attributes, or the nature of health problems.
1.1 Respect for Human Dignity
The fundamental principle of nursing practice is respect for the inherent dignity and worth of every client. Nurses are morally obligated to respect human existence and the individuality of all persons who are the recipients of nursing actions. Nurses therefore must take all reasonable means to protect and preserve human life when there is hope of recovery or reasonable hope of benefit from life-prolonging treatment.

Truth telling and the process of reaching informed choice underlie the exercise of self-determination, which is basic to respect for persons. Clients should be as fully involved as possible in the planning and implementation of their own health care. Clients have the moral right to determine what will be done with their own person; to be given accurate information, and all the information necessary for making informed judgments; to be assisted with weighing the benefits and burdens of options in their treatment; accept, refuse, or terminate treatment without coercion; and to be given necessary emotional support. Each nurse has an obligation to be knowledgeable about the moral and legal rights of all clients and to protect and support those rights. In situations in which the client lacks the capacity to make a decision, a surrogate decision maker should be designated.

Individuals are interdependent members of the community. Taking into account both individual rights and the interdependence of persons in decision making, the nurse recognizes those situations in which individual rights to autonomy in health care may temporarily be overridden to preserve the life of the human community; for example, when a disaster demands triage or when an individual presents a direct danger to others. The many variables involved make it imperative that each case be considered with full awareness of the need to preserve the rights and responsibilities of clients and the demands of justice. The suspension of individual rights must always be considered a deviation to be tolerated as briefly as possible.

1.2 Status and Attributes of Clients

The need for health care is universal, transcending all national, ethnic, racial, religious, cultural, political, educational, economic, developmental, personality, role, and sexual differences. Nursing care is delivered without prejudicial behavior. Individual value systems and life-styles should be considered in the planning of health care with and for each client. Attributes of clients influence nursing practice to the extent that they represent factors the nurse must understand, consider, and respect in tailoring care to personal needs and in maintaining the individual's self-respect and dignity.

1.3 The Nature of Health Problems

The nurse's respect for the worth and dignity of the individual human being applies, irrespective of the nature of the health problem. It is reflected in care given the person who is disabled as well as one without disability, the person with long-term illness as well as one with acute illness, the recovering patient as well as one in the last phase of life. This respect extends to all who require the services of the nurse for the promotion of health, the prevention of illness, the restoration of health, the alleviation of suffering, and the provision of supportive care of the dying. The nurse does not act deliberately to terminate the life of any person.

The nurse's concern for human dignity and for the provision of high quality nursing care is not limited by personal attitudes or beliefs. If ethically opposed to interventions in a particular case because of the procedures to be used, the nurse is justified in refusing to participate. Such refusal should be made known in advance and in time for other appropriate arrangements to be made for the client's nursing care. If the nurse becomes involved in such a case and the client's life is in jeopardy, the nurse is obliged to provide for the client's safety, to avoid abandonment, and to withdraw only when assured that alternative sources of nursing care are available to the client.

The measures nurses take to care for the dying client and the client's family emphasize human contact. They enable the client to live with as much physical, emotional, and spiritual comfort as possible, and they maximize the values the client has treasured in life. Nursing care is directed toward the prevention and relief of the suffering commonly associated with the dying process. The nurse may provide interventions to relieve symptoms in the dying client even when the interventions entail substantial risks of hastening death.

1.4 The Setting for Health Care

The nurse adheres to the principle of nondiscriminatory, nonprejudicial care in every situation and endeavors to promote its acceptance by others. The setting shall not determine the nurse's readiness to respect clients and to render or obtain needed services.

2 The nurse safeguards the client's right to privacy by judiciously protecting information of a confidential nature.

2.1 The Client's Right to Privacy

The right to privacy is an inalienable human right. The client trusts the nurse to hold all information in confidence. This trust could be destroyed and the client's welfare jeopardized by injudicious disclosure of information provided in confidence. The duty of confidentiality, however, is not absolute when innocent parties are in direct jeopardy.

2.2 Protection of Information

The rights, well-being, and safety of the individual client should be the determining factors in arriving at any professional judgment concerning the disposition of confidential information received from the client relevant to his or her treatment. The standards of nursing practice and the nursing responsibility to provide high quality health services require that relevant data be shared with members of the health team. Only information pertinent to a client's treatment and welfare is disclosed, and it is disclosed only to those directly concerned with the client's care.

Information documenting the appropriateness, necessity, and quality of care required for the purposes of peer review, third-party payment, and other quality assurance mechanisms must be disclosed only under defined policies, mandates, or protocols. These written guidelines must assure that the rights, well-being, and safety of the client are maintained.

2.3 Access to Records

If in the course of providing care there is a need for the nurse to have access to the records of persons not under the nurse's care, the persons affected should be notified and, whenever possible permission should be obtained first. Although records belong to the agency where the data are collected, the individual maintains the right of control over the information in the record. Similarly, professionals may exercise the right of control over information they have generated in the course of health care.

If the nurse wishes to use a client's treatment record for research or non-clinical purposes in which anonymity cannot be guaranteed, the client's consent must be obtained first. Ethically, this ensures the client's right to privacy; legally, it protects the client against unlawful invasion of privacy.

3 The nurse acts to safeguard the client and the public when health care and safety are affected by incompetent, unethical, or illegal practice by any person.

3.1 Safeguarding the Health and Safety of the Client
The nurse's primary commitment is to the health, welfare, and safety of the client. As an advocate for the client, the nurse must be alert to and take appropriate action regarding any instances of incompetent, unethical, or illegal practice by any member of the health care team or the health care system, or any action on the part of others that places the rights or best interests of the client in jeopardy. To function effectively in this role, nurses must be aware of the employing institution's policies and procedures, nursing standards of practice, the Code for Nurses, and laws governing nursing and health care practice with regard to incompetent, unethical, or illegal practice.

3.2 Acting on Questionable Practice
When the nurse is aware of inappropriate or questionable practice in the provision of health care, concern should be expressed to the person carrying out the questionable practice and attention called to the possible detrimental effect upon the client's welfare. When factors in the health care delivery system threaten the welfare of the client, similar action should be directed to the responsible administrative person. If indicated, the practice should then be reported to the appropriate authority within the institution, agency, or larger system.

There should be an established process for the reporting and handling of incompetent, unethical, or illegal practice within the employment setting so that such reporting can go through official channels without causing fear of reprisal. The nurse should be knowledgeable about the process and be prepared to use it if necessary. When questions are raised about the practices of individual practitioners or of health care systems, written documentation of the observed practices or behaviors must be available to the appropriate authorities. State nurses' associations should be prepared to provide assistance and support in the development and evaluation of such processes and in reporting procedures.

When incompetent, unethical, or illegal practice on the part of anyone concerned with the client's care is not corrected within the employment setting and continues to jeopardize the client's welfare and safety, the problem should be reported to other appropriate authorities such as practice committees of the pertinent professional organizations or the legally constituted bodies concerned with licensing of specific categories of health workers or professional practitioners. Some situations may warrant the concern and involvement of all such groups. Accurate reporting and documentation undergird all actions.

3.3 Review Mechanisms

The nurse should participate in the planning, establishment, implementation, and evaluation of review mechanisms that serve to safeguard clients, such as duly constituted peer review processes or committees and ethics committees. Such ongoing review mechanisms are based on established criteria, have stated purposes, include a process for making recommendations, and facilitate improved delivery of nursing and other health services to clients wherever nursing services are provided.

4 The nurse assumes responsibility and accountability for individual nursing judgments and actions.

4.1 Acceptance of Responsibility and Accountability

The recipients of professional nursing services are entitled to high quality nursing care. Individual professional licensure is the protective mechanism legislated by the public to ensure the basic and minimum competencies of the professional nurse. Beyond that, society has accorded to the nursing profession the right to regulate its own practice. The regulation and control of nursing practice by nurses demand that individual practitioners of professional nursing must bear primary responsibility for the nursing care clients receive and must be individually accountable for their own practice.

4.2 Responsibility for Nursing Judgment and Action

Responsibility refers to the carrying out of duties associated with a particular role assumed by the nurse. Nursing obligations are reflected in the ANA publications *Nursing: A Social Policy Statement* and *Standards of Nursing Practice*. In recognizing the rights of clients, the standards describe a collaborative relationship between the nurse and the client through use of the nursing process. Nursing responsibilities include data collection and assessment of the health status of the client; formation of nursing diagnoses derived from client assessment; development of a nursing care plan that is directed toward designated goals, assists the client in maximizing his or her health capabilities, and provides for the client's participation in promoting, maintaining, and restoring his or her health; evaluation of the effectiveness of nursing care in achieving goals as determined by the client and the nurse; and subsequent reassessment and revision of the nursing care plan as warranted. In the process of assuming these responsibilities, the nurse is held accountable for them.

4.3 Accountability for Nursing Judgment and Action

Accountability refers to being answerable to someone for something one has done. It means providing an explanation or rationale to oneself, to clients, to peers, to the nursing profession, and to society. In order to be accountable, nurses act under a code of ethical conduct that is grounded in the moral principles of fidelity and respect for the dignity, worth, and self-determination of clients.

The nursing profession continues to develop ways to clarify nursing's accountability to society. The contract between the profession and society is made explicit through such mechanisms as (a) the Code for Nurses, (b) the standards of nursing practice, (c) the development of nursing theory derived from nursing research in order to guide nursing actions, (d) educational requirements for practice, (e) certification, and (f) mechanisms for evaluating the effectiveness of the nurse's performance of nursing responsibilities.

Nurses are accountable for judgments made and actions taken in the course of nursing practice. Neither physicians' orders nor the employing agency's policies relieve the nurse of accountability for actions taken and judgments made.

5 The nurse maintains competence in nursing.

5.1 Personal Responsibility for Competence

The profession of nursing is obligated to provide adequate and competent nursing care. Therefore it is the personal responsibility of each nurse to maintain competency in practice. For the client's optimum well-being and for the nurse's own professional development, the care of the client reflects and incorporates new techniques and knowledge in health care as these develop, especially as they relate to the nurse's particular field of practice. The nurse must be aware of the need for continued professional learning and must assume personal responsibility for currency of knowledge and skills.

5.2 Measurement of Competence in Nursing Practice

Evaluation of one's performance by peers is a hallmark of professionalism and a method by which the profession is held accountable to society. Nurses must be willing to have their practice reviewed and evaluated by their peers. Guidelines for evaluating the scope of practice and the appropriateness, effectiveness, and efficiency of nursing practice are found in nursing practice acts, ANA standards of practice, and other quality assurance mechanisms. Each nurse is responsible for participating in the development of objective criteria for evaluation. In addition, the nurse engages in ongoing self-evaluation of clinical competency, decision-making abilities, and professional judgments.

5.3 Intraprofessional Responsibility for Competence in Nursing Care
Nurses share responsibility for high quality nursing care. Nurses are required to have knowledge relevant to the current scope of nursing practice, changing issues and concerns, and ethical concepts and principles. Since individual competencies vary, nurses refer clients to and consult with other nurses with expertise and recognized competencies in various fields of practice.

6 The nurse exercises informed judgment and uses individual competency and qualifications as criteria in seeking consultation, accepting responsibilities, and delegating nursing activities.
6.1 Changing Functions
Nurses are faced with decisions in the context of the increased complexity of health care, changing patterns in the delivery of health services, and the development of evolving nursing practice in response to the health needs of clients. As the scope of nursing practice changes, the nurse must exercise judgment in accepting responsibilities, seeking consultation, and assigning responsibilities to others who carry out nursing care.

6.2 Accepting Responsibilities
The nurse must not engage in practices prohibited by law or delegate to others activities prohibited by practice acts of other health care personnel or by other laws. Nurses determine the scope of their practice in light of their education, knowledge, competency, and extent of experience. If the nurse concludes that he or she lacks competence or is inadequately prepared to carry out a specific function, the nurse has the responsibility to refuse that work and to seek alternative sources of care based on concern for the client's welfare. In that refusal, both the client and the nurse are protected. Inasmuch as the nurse is responsible for the continuous care of patients in health care settings, the nurse is frequently called upon to carry out components of care delegated by other health professionals as part of the client's treatment regimen. The nurse should not accept these interdependent functions if they are so extensive as to prevent the nurse from fulfilling the responsibility to provide appropriate nursing care to clients.

6.3 Consultation and Collaboration

The provision of health and illness care to clients is a complex process that requires a wide range of knowledge, skills, and collaborative efforts. Nurses must be aware of their own individual competencies. When the needs of the client are beyond the qualifications and competencies of the nurse, consultation and collaboration must be sought from qualified nurses, other health professionals, or other appropriate sources. Participation on intradisciplinary or interdisciplinary teams is often an effective approach to the provision of high quality total health services.

6.4 Delegation of Nursing Activities

Inasmuch as the nurse is accountable for the quality of nursing care rendered to clients, nurses are accountable for the delegation of nursing care activities to other health workers. Therefore, the nurse must assess individual competency in assigning selected components of nursing care to other nursing service personnel. The nurse should not delegate to any member of the nursing team a function for which that person is not prepared or qualified. Employer policies or directives do not relieve the nurse of accountability for making judgments about the delegation of nursing care activities.

7 The nurse participates in activities that contribute to the ongoing development of the profession's body of knowledge.

7.1 The Nurse and Development of Knowledge

Every profession must engage in scholarly inquiry to identify, verify, and continually enlarge the body of knowledge that forms the foundation for its practice. A unique body of verified knowledge provides both framework and direction for the profession in all of its activities and for the practitioner in the provision of nursing care. The accrual of scientific and humanistic knowledge promotes the advancement of practice and the well-being of the profession's clients. Ongoing scholarly activity such as research and the development of theory is indispensable to the full discharge of a profession's obligations to society. Each nurse has a role in this area of professional activity, whether as an investigator in furthering knowledge, as a participant in research, or as a user of theoretical and empirical knowledge.

7.2 Protection of Rights of Human Participants in Research

Individual rights valued by society and by the nursing profession that have particular application in research include the right of adequately informed consent, the right to freedom from risk of injury, and the right of privacy and preservation of dignity. Inherent in these rights is respect for each individual's rights to exercise self-determination, to choose to participate or not, to have full information, and to terminate participation in research without penalty.

It is the duty of the nurse functioning in any research role to maintain vigilance in protecting the life, health, and privacy of human subjects from both anticipated and unanticipated risks and in assuring informed consent. Subjects' integrity, privacy, and rights must be especially safeguarded if the subjects are unable to protect themselves because of incapacity or because they are in a dependent relationship to the investigator. The investigation should be discontinued if its continuance might be harmful to the subject.

7.3 General Guidelines for Participating in Research

Before participating in research conducted by others, the nurse has an obligation to (a) obtain information about the intent and the nature of the research and (b) ascertain that the study proposal is approved by the appropriate bodies, such as institutional review boards.

Research should be conducted and directed by qualified persons. The nurse who participates in research in any capacity should be fully informed about both the nurse's and the client's rights and obligations.

8 The nurse participates in the profession's efforts to implement and improve standards of nursing.

8.1 Responsibility to the Public for Standards

Nursing is responsible and accountable for admitting to the profession only those individuals who have demonstrated the knowledge, skills, and commitment considered essential to professional practice. Nurse educators have a major responsibility for ensuring that these competencies and a demonstrated commitment to professional practice have been achieved before the entry of an individual into the practice of professional nursing.

Established standards and guidelines for nursing practice provide guidance for the delivery of professional nursing care and are a means for evaluating care received by the public. The nurse has a personal responsibility and commitment to clients for implementation and maintenance of optimal standards of nursing practice.

8.2 Responsibility to the Profession for Standards

Established standards reflect the practice of nursing grounded in ethical commitments and a body of knowledge. Professional standards or guidelines exist in nursing practice, nursing service, nursing education, and nursing research. The nurse has the responsibility to monitor these standards in daily practice and to participate actively in the profession's ongoing efforts to foster optimal standards of practice at the local, regional, state, and national levels of the health care system.

Nurse educators have the additional responsibility to maintain optimal standards of nursing practice and education in nursing education programs and in any other settings where planned learning activities for nursing students take place.

9 The nurse participates in the profession's efforts to establish and maintain conditions of employment conducive to high quality nursing care.

9.1 Responsibility for Conditions of Employment

The nurse must be concerned with conditions of employment that (a) enable the nurse to practice in accordance with the standards of nursing practice and (b) provide a care environment that meets the standards of nursing service. The provision of high quality nursing care is the responsibility of both the individual nurse and the nursing profession. Professional autonomy and self-regulation in the control of conditions of practice are necessary for implementing nursing standards.

9.2 Maintaining Conditions for High Quality Nursing Care

Articulation and control of nursing practice can be accomplished through individual agreement and collective action. A nurse may enter into an agreement with individuals or organizations to provide health care.

Nurses may participate in collective action such as collective bargaining through their state nurses' association to determine the terms and conditions of employment conducive to high quality nursing care. Such agreements should be consistent with the profession's standards of practice, the state law regulating nursing practice, and the Code for Nurses.

10 The nurse participates in the profession's effort to protect the public from misinformation and misrepresentation and to maintain the integrity of nursing.

10.1 Protection from Misinformation and Misrepresentation

Nurses are responsible for advising clients against the use of products that endanger the clients' safety and welfare. The nurse shall not use any form of public or professional communication to make claims that are false, fraudulent, misleading, deceptive, or unfair. The nurse does not give or imply endorsement to advertising, promotion, or sale of commercial products or services in a manner that may be interpreted as reflecting the opinion or judgment of the profession as a whole. The nurse may use knowledge of specific services or products in advising an individual client, since this may contribute to the client's health and well-being. In the course of providing information or education to clients or other practitioners about commercial products or services, however, a variety of similar products or services should be offered or described so the client or practitioner can make an informed choice.

10.2 Maintaining the Integrity of Nursing

The use of the title registered nurse is granted by state governments for the protection of the public. Use of that title carries with it the responsibility to act in the public interest. The nurse may use the title R.N. and symbols of academic degrees or other earned or honorary professional symbols of recognition in all ways that are legal and appropriate. The title and other symbols of the profession should not be used, however, for benefits unrelated to nursing practice or the profession, or used by those who may seek to exploit them for other purposes.

Nurses should refrain from casting a vote in any deliberations involving health care services or facilities where the nurse has business or other interests that could be construed as a conflict of interest.

11 The nurse collaborates with members of the health professions and other citizens in promoting community and national efforts to meet the health needs of the public.

11.1 Collaboration with Others to Meet Health Needs

The availability and accessibility of high quality health services to all people require collaborative planning at the local, state, national, and international levels that respects the interdependence of health professionals and clients in health care systems. Nursing care is an integral part of high quality health care, and nurses have an obligation to promote equitable access to nursing and health care for all people.

11.2 Responsibility to the Public

The nursing profession is committed to promoting the welfare and safety of all people. The goals and values of nursing are essential to effective delivery of health services. For the benefit of the individual client and the public at large, nursing's goals and commitments need adequate representation. Nurses should ensure this representation by active participation in decision making in institutional and political arenas to assure a just distribution of health care and nursing resource.

11.3 Relationships with Other Disciplines

The complexity of health care delivery systems requires a multidisciplinary approach to delivery of services that has the strong support and active participation of all the health professions. Nurses should actively promote the collaborative planning required to ensure the availability and accessibility of high quality health services to all persons whose health needs are unmet.

Committee on Ethics, 1983-1985
Catherine P. Murphy, Ed.D., R.N., chairperson
Mila A. Aroskar, Ed.D., R.N., F.A.A.N.
Sister Karin Dufault, Ph.D., R.N.
Carol A. Jenkins, M.S.N., R.N.
Marilyn Whipple, M.S., R.N., C.S.

Committee on Ethics, 1981-1982
Anne J. Davis, Ph.D., R.N., F.A.A.N., chairperson
Carol A. Jenkins, M.S.N., R.N.
Catherine P. Murphy, Ed.D., R.N.
Rita J. Payton, P.A., R.N.
Joyce Thompson, Dr. P. H., R.N., F.A.A.N.

APPENDIX D:
ESSENTIALS OF COLLEGE AND UNIVERSITY EDUCATION FOR PROFESSIONAL NURSING

Final Report (pages 4-7)

American Association of Colleges of Nursing
One Dupont Circle, Suite 530
Washington, D.C. 20036

Liberal Education

In 1984 and 1985, three national panels recommended improvements for the undergraduate curriculum, especially in liberal education (Association of American Colleges, 1985; National Institute of Education, 1984; and National Endowment for the Humanities, 1984). **We recommend that the education of the professional nurse reflect the spirit of these reports so that the graduate will exhibit qualities of mind and character that are necessary to live a free and fulfilling life, act in the public interest locally and globally, and contribute to health care improvements and the nursing profession.** The aim of education is to prepare a fully-functioning human being. A major nursing function is to enhance the well-being of others, therefore, the nurse must have the educational foundation to foster personal well-being and continuing growth.

Knowledge is neither the exclusive province of the experts in an academic discipline nor limited to a specific set of courses. The whole academic community shares responsibility for the education of the student. Knowledge acquired at the college or university level builds on previous experience and learning and is enhanced by collaboration among faculty from many disciplines. The liberally educated person who is prepared in this manner can responsibly challenge the status quo and anticipate and adapt to change.

We recommend that the education of the professional nurse ensure the ability to:

1. Write, read, and speak English clearly and effectively in order to acquire knowledge, convey and discuss ideas, evaluate information, and think critically.

2. Think analytically and reason logically using verifiable information and past experience in order to select or create solutions to problems.

3. Understand a second language, at least at an elementary level, in order to widen access to the diversity of world cultures.

4. Understand other cultural traditions in order to gain a perspective on personal values and the similarities and differences among individuals and groups.

5. Use mathematical concepts, interpret quantitative data, and use computers and other information technology in order to analyze problems and develop positions that depend on numbers and statistics.

6. Use concepts from the behavioral and biological sciences in order to understand oneself and one's relationships with other people and to comprehend the nature and function of communities.

7. Understand the physical world and its interrelationship with human activity in order to make decisions that are based on scientific evidence and responsive to the values and interests of the individual and society.

8. Comprehend life and time from historical and contemporary perspectives and draw from past experiences to influence the present and future.

9. Gain a perspective on social, political, and economic issues for resolving societal and professional problems.

10. Comprehend the meaning of human spirituality in order to recognize the relationship of beliefs to culture, behavior, health, and healing.

11. Appreciate the role of the fine and performing arts in stimulating individual creativity, expressing personal feelings and emotions, and building a sense of the commonality of human experience.

12. Understand the nature of human values and develop a personal philosophy in order to make ethical judgments in both personal and professional life.

Professors of nursing, like all faculty, must help shape and actively support the liberal education requirements of their colleges and universities. Nursing faculty are responsible for integrating knowledge from the liberal arts and sciences into professional nursing education and practice. Liberally educated nurses make informed and responsible ethical choices and help shape the future of society as well as the nursing profession.

Values and Professional Behaviors

College and university education for professional nursing includes processes that foster the development of values, attitudes, personal qualities, and professional behaviors. Values are defined as beliefs or ideals to which an individual is committed and which guide behavior. Values are reflected in attitudes, personal qualities, and consistent patterns of behavior. Attitudes are inclinations or dispositions to respond positively or negatively to a person, object, or situation, while personal qualities are innate or learned attributes of an individual. Professional behaviors reflect the individual's commitment to specific values.

Nursing has been described as a cultural paradox. The professional nurse must adopt contemporary characteristics such as independence, assertiveness, self-esteem, and confidence as well as those of a more traditional nature such as compassion, acceptance, consideration, and kindness. Adoption of the essential values leads the nurse to a sense of commitment and social responsibility, a sensitivity and responsiveness to the needs of others, and a responsibility for oneself and one's actions.

We recommend that the following seven values are essential for the professional nurse. Examples of attitudes, personal qualities and professional behaviors are included that reflect a commitment to one or more of these values.

Essential Values*	Examples of Attitudes and Personal Qualities	Examples of Professional Behaviors
1. ALTRUISM Concern for the welfare of others.	Caring Commitment Compassion Generosity Perseverance	Gives full attention to the patient/client when giving care. Assists other personnel in providing care when they are unable to do so. Expresses concern about social trends and issues that have implications for health care.

2. EQUALITY
Having the same rights, privileges, or status.

Acceptance
Assertiveness
Fairness
Self-esteem
Tolerance

Provides nursing care based on the individual's needs irrespective of personal characteristics.**
  Interacts with other providers in a non-discriminatory manner.
  Expresses ideas about the improvement of access to nursing and health care.

3. ESTHETICS
Qualities of objects, events, and persons that provide satisfaction.

Appreciation
Creativity
Imagination
Sensitivity

Adapts the environment so it is pleasing to the patient/client.
  Creates a pleasant work environment for self and others.
  Presents self in a manner that promotes a positive image of nursing.

4. FREEDOM
Capacity to exercise choice.

Confidence
Hope
Independence
Openness
Self-direction
Self-discipline

Honors individual's right to refuse treatment.
  Supports the rights of other providers to suggest alternatives to the plan of care.
  Encourages open discussion of controversial issues in the profession.

5. HUMAN DIGNITY
Inherent worth and uniqueness of an individual.

Consideration
Empathy
Humaneness
Kindness
Respectfulness
Trust

Safeguards the individual's right to privacy.
  Addresses individuals as they prefer to be addressed.
  Maintains confidentiality of patients/clients and staff.
  Treats others with respect regardless of background.

6. JUSTICE
Upholding moral and legal principles.

Courage
Integrity
Morality
Objectivity

Acts as a health care advocate.
  Allocates resources fairly.
  Reports incompetent, unethical, and illegal practice objectively and factually.**

7. TRUTH
Faithfulness to fact or
reality.

Accountability
Authenticity
Honesty
Inquisitiveness
Rationality
Reflectiveness

Documents nursing care accurately
and honestly.
  Obtains sufficient data to make
sound judgments before reporting
infractions of organizational
policies.
  Participates in professional
efforts to protect the public from
misinformation about nursing.

* The values are listed in alphabetic rather than priority order.
** From *Code for Nurses*. American Nurses' Association, 1976.

The professional nurse assigns priorities to these values within specific
decision-making contexts in the application of essential knowledge and practice. The nurse, guided by these values, attitudes, and personal qualities,
demonstrates ethical professional behavior with patients/clients, colleagues,
and others in providing safe, humanistic care focused on health and quality
of life. Values, attitudes, personal qualities, and consistent patterns of
behavior begin to develop early in life, but also are fostered and facilitated
by selected educational strategies and the process of socialization to the
profession.

Notes

Chapter One: Personal Values

[1]Diann Uustal, "The Use of Values in Nursing Practice," in *The Journal of Continuing Education in Nursing* (8:3) 1977, p. 9.

[2]Judith Allen Shelly, *The Spiritual Needs of Children* (Downers Grove, Ill.: InterVarsity Press, 1982), p. 54.

[3]Charlotte A. Aikens, R.N., *Studies in Ethics for Nurses* (Philadelphia and London: W. B. Saunders Company, 1923) pp. 65-71.

[4]Martin E. Marty and Kenneth L. Vaux, *Health/Medicine and the Faith Traditions* (Philadelphia: Fortress Press, 1982), p. 223.

[5]Madalon O'Rawe Amenta and Nancy L. Bohnet, *Nursing Care of the Terminally Ill* (Boston/Toronto: Little, Brown and Company, 1986), p. 142.

[6]Lesslie Newbigin, *Foolishness to the Greeks* (Grand Rapids, Mich.: Eerdmans, 1986) pp. 65-71.

Chapter Two: A Case for Value Judgments

[1]Edward H. Jennings, *Essentials of College and University Education for Professional Nursing: Final Report,* American Association of Colleges of Nursing (AACN), 1986.

[2]Sigmund Freud, *A General Introduction to Psychoanalysis* (New York: Liveright Publishing Corporation, 1924).

[3]William Glassner. M.D., *Reality Therapy* (New York: Harper and Row, 1965).

Chapter 3: Assessing Your Values

[1]Diann Uustal, *Values and Ethics in Nursing: From Theory to Practice* (East Greenwich, R.I.: Educational Resources in Nursing and Holistic Health,

1985), p. 99.

[2]Stanley Hauerwas and William H. Willimon, "Peculiar People," *Christianity Today,* March 5, 1990, p. 16. Excerpt from the book *Resident Aliens: Life in the Christian Colony* by the same authors (Nashville/New York: Abingdon Press, 1989).

Chapter Four: A History of Nursing Values

[1]Mary Jane Shank, Ph.D., and Darlene Weis, RN, MSN, "A Study of Values of Baccalaureate Nursing Students and Graduate Nurses from a Secular and Nonsecular Program," *Journal of Professional Nursing,* 5(1), January-February, 1989, pp. 17-22.

[2]Margaret A. Williams, Dorothy W. Bloch and Eunice M. Blair, "Values and Value Changes of Graduate Nursing Students: Their Relationship to Faculty Values and to Selected Educational Factors," *Nursing Research,* 27(3), May/June 1978, pp. 181-89.

[3]Marlene Kramer, *Reality Shock: Why Nurses Leave Nursing* (St. Louis: C. V. Mosby Company, 1974), pp. 1-66.

[4]Kay B. Partridge, "Nursing Values in a Changing Society," *Nursing Outlook,* June 1978, p. 357.

[5]Charles Dickens, *Martin Chuzzlewit* (New York/Boston: Books, Inc., 1868). Mrs. Gamp is introduced in chapter nineteen and continues as a key figure for the remainder of the book.

[6]American Nurses Association, "Code for Nurses," statement number 9.

[7]Mary Lewis Coakley, "Florence Nightingale, a One-Woman Revolution," *Journal of Christian Nursing,* 6(1), Winter 1989, p. 22.

[8]Leslie D. Atkinson and Mary Ellen Murray, *Fundamentals of Nursing, A Nursing Process Approach,* New York: Macmillan, 1985), p. 7.

[9]Mary E. Gladwin, *Ethics: A Textbook for Nurses* (Philadelphia and London: W. B. Saunders Company, 1937), p. 328.

[10]Coakley, *Christian Nursing,* p. 22.

[11]Donna H. Groh, "Treatment of Torture: Why Critical Care?" in Marsha D. M. Fowler and June Levine-Ariff, *Ethics at the Bedside* (Philadelphia: Lippincott, 1987), pp. 4-5.

[12]Leah Curtain and M. Josephine Flaherty, *Nursing Ethics: Theories and Pragmatics* (Bowie, Md.: Robert J. Brady Co., 1982), p. 141.

[13]See almost any early nursing text, including Gladwin, *Textbook for Nurses,* and Charlotte A. Aikens, *Studies in Ethics for Nurses* (Philadelphia and London: W. B. Saunders, 1916).

[14]Allen Verhey, "The Doctor's Oath—and a Christian Swearing It," in Stephen E. Lammers and Allen Verhey, eds., *On Moral Medicine: Theological*

Perspectives in Medical Ethics (Grand Rapids, Mich.: Eerdmans, 1987), p. 73.

[15]Rita L. Marker, "Euthanasia: The New Family Planning, Part I," *International Review of Natural Family Planning*, 11(1), Spring 1987, pp. 1-31.

[16]Robert A. Derzon, "Additional Cost-Saving Initiatives—ACTION," *Memorandum, Department of Health, Education and Welfare* (Health Care Financing and Administration), OPPR: CGaus: 6/3/77: X50681, p. 6.

[17]Gladwin, *Textbook for Nurses*, p. 272.

[18]For an example of how one nurse challenged a State Nurses Association's endorsement of abortion, see Molly K. Linder, "I Challenged the State Nurses Association," *Journal of Christian Nursing*, 5(1), Winter 1988, pp. 16-19.

[19]See James L. Muyskens, "Acting Alone," *American Journal of Nursing*, 87(9), September 1987, p. 1141.

[20]Dickens, *Martin Chuzzlewit*, p. 318.

[21]Dorothy Emmet, "Professional Ethics," in James F. Childress and John Macquarrie, eds., *The Westminster Dictionary of Christian Ethics* (Philadelphia: Westminster Press, 1986), p. 502.

[22]Emmet, "Professional Ethics," p. 502.

[23]Aikens, *Studies in Ethics*, pp. 227-28.

[24]Verhey, "The Doctor's Oath," p. 76.

[25]Gladwin, *Textbook for Nurses*, pp. 223-24.

[26]Atkinson and Murray, *Fundamentals of Nursing*, p. 5.

[27]Coakley, *Christian Nursing*, pp. 23-24.

[28]Partridge, *Nursing Outlook*, p. 357.

[29]"A Suggested Code," *American Journal of Nursing*, August 1926, pp. 599-601.

[30]"A Code for Nurses," *American Journal of Nursing*, April 1950, p. 196.

[31]Diane C. Viens, "A History of Nursing's Code of Ethics," *Nursing Outlook*, 37(1), January-February 1989, p. 48.

[32]*Code for Nurses With Interpretive Statements*, American Nurses Association, 2420 Pershing Road, Kansas City, MO 64108, G-56 12M 7/85.

[33]Viens, *Code of Ethics*, p. 49.

[34]Edward H. Jennings, *Essentials of College and University Education for Professional Nursing, Final Report*, American Association of Colleges of Nursing, 1986, pp. 6-7.

[35]Robert S. Brumbaugh, "Aristotle," *Funk and Wagnalls New Encyclopedia*, Vol. 2, p. 328.

Chapter Five: Values in Today's Nursing

[1]Demographics of survey respondents closely matched those reported in the American Nurses Association's "Registered Nurse Fact Sheet: based on a

national survey in 1984."

[2]Sharon Fish, "From Florence to Athens: Nursing's New Age," *SCP Newsletter* (14:3) 1989, pp. 1, 3-8.

[3]Donald Posterski, *Reinventing Evangelism* (Downers Grove, Ill.: InterVarsity Press, 1989), pp. 66-67.

[4]Mila Ann Aroskar, "Are Nurses' Mind Sets Compatible with Ethical Practice?" *Topics in Clinical Nursing* (April 1982), p. 22.

[5]Posterski, *Reinventing Evangelism*, p. 69.

[6]A non-parametric analysis of variance (Kruskal-Wallis test) showed the following results (scaled to a mean of 0 and a standard deviation of 1) of the personal value of power: Dipl-Bacc 2.52**, Dipl-Master 4.31*, Bacc-Master 2.24*. (**significant at the 0.05 level; *significant at the 0.10 level).

[7]Kruskal-Wallis deviation of 2.81**.

[8]K. R. Stevens, *Power and Influence: A Sourcebook for Nurses* (New York: Wiley and Sons, 1983).

[9]American Nurses' Association, *Bylaws* (Kansas City, MO, 1980).

[10]International Council of Nurses, Geneva, Switzerland, in L. D. Atkinson and M. E. Murray, *Fundamentals of Nursing: A Nursing Process Approach* (New York: Macmillan, 1985), p. 14.

[11]C. A. Wynd, "Packing a Punch: Female Nurses and the Effective Use of Power," *Nursing Success Today*, 2(9), pp. 15-20.

[12]Mary Mallison, "Everyday Visionaries," *American Journal of Nursing*, October 1989, p. 1259.

[13]Barbara Simsen, "In Perspective," *Christian Nurse International*, 5(4), 1989, p. 3.

[14]Kim Young In (translator), "Surprised by Tears," *Christian Nurse International*, 5(4), 1989, pp. 6-7.

[15]Simsen, "In Perspective."

Chapter Six: Foundations for Christian Values

[1]Diann B. Uustal, "Values: the Cornerstone of Nursing's Moral Art," Chapter 9 in Marsha D. M. Fowler and June Levine-Ariff, eds., *Ethics at the Bedside* (Philadelphia: J. B. Lippincott Co., 1987), pp. 149-50.

[2]Earl D. Wilson, *Counseling and Homosexuality* (Waco, Tex.: Word, 1988), p. 21.

[3]Gail C. Davis, "Nursing Values and Health Care Policy," *Nursing Outlook*, November/ December 1988, pp. 289-92.

[4]Donald B. Kraybill and Phyllis Pellman Good, eds., *Perils of Professionalism* (Scottdale, Penn.:Herald Press, 1982), p. 227.

[5]Lewis B. Smedes, *Mere Morality* (Grand Rapids, Mich.: Eerdmans, 1983), pp. 1-2.

[6]Uustal, "Values," p. 145.

[7]John Keinig, "A Libertarian Response to Moral Diversity," *Hastings Center Report*, February 1987, pp. 34-35. (A review of Engelhardt's book.)

[8]Seymour B. Sarason, "And What Is the Public Interest?" *American Psychologist* (41:8) August 1986, p. 899.

[9]James W. Sire, *The Universe Next Door*, 2nd edition (Downers Grove, Ill.: InterVarsity, 1988), p. 26.

[10]Clark Pinnock, "Revelation," in Sinclair B. Ferguson, David F. Wright and J. I. Packer, eds., *New Dictionary of Theology* (Downers Grove, Ill.: InterVarsity Press, 1988), p. 585.

[11]Smedes, *Mere Morality*, p. 22.

[12]Margaret Joan Fromer, *Ethical Issues in Health Care* (St. Louis: C. V. Mosby Co., 1981) p. 20.

[13]Clark Pinnock, "Revelation," in Ferguson et al., *Dictionary of Theology*, pp. 586-87.

[14]Sire, *Universe Next Door*, p. 40.

[15]Beth Spring and Ed Larson, *Euthanasia: Spiritual, Medical and Legal Issues in Terminal Health Care* (Portland: Multnomah Press, 1989), p. 122.

[16]Stanley Hauerwas, *Suffering Presence* (Notre Dame, Ind.: University of Notre Dame Press, 1986), p. 25.

Chapter Seven: Nursing Values and Christian Character

[1]Dorothy E. Reilly, *Teaching and Evaluation: the Affective Domain in Nursing Programs* (Thorofare, N.J.: Charles B. Slack, 1987), pp. 50-51.

[2]For example, see Robert M. Veatch and Sara T. Fry, *Case Studies in Nursing Ethics* (Philadelphia: Lippincott, 1987) and Marsha D. M. Fowler and June Levine-Ariff, *Ethics at the Bedside* (Philadelphia: Lippincott, 1987).

[3]Marsha D. Fowler, "Ethics Without Virtue," *Heart and Lung* (15:5), September 1986, p. 529.

[4]"Essentials of College and University Education For Professional Nursing," **Final Report** (Washington, D.C.: American Association of Colleges of Nursing, 1986), pp. 5-7.

[5]Fowler, "Ethics Without Virtue," p. 529.

[6]"Essentials," *Final Report*, p. 7.

[7]For example, see Roland R. Yarling and Beverly J. McElmurry, "The Moral Foundation of Nursing," *Advances in Nursing Science* (8:2, 1986), pp. 63-73.

[8]Stanley Hauerwas, *The Peaceable Kingdom: A Primer in Christian Ethics* (Notre Dame: University Press, 1983), p. 39.

[9]Hauerwas, *The Peaceable Kingdom*, p. 42.

[10]William Glasser, *Reality Therapy: A New Approach to Psychiatry* (New York:

Harper and Row, 1965).

[11]Donna Diers, "Learning the Art and Craft of Nursing," *American Journal of Nursing,* January 1990, p. 64.

[12]Michael Griffiths, *The Example of Jesus* (Downers Grove, Ill.: InterVarsity Press, 1985), p. 44.

[13]Josephine A. Dolan, M. Louise Fitzpatrick, and Eleanor Krohn Herrman, *Nursing in Society: A Historical Perspective,* 15th edition (Philadelphia: W. B. Saunders, 1983).

[14]Everett L. Wilson, "When Mercy Becomes a Business," *Christianity Today,* February 19, 1990, p. 23.

Chapter Nine: A Strategy for Influence

[1]Stephen Charles Mott, *Biblical Ethics and Social Change* (New York: Oxford University Press, 1982), p. 52.

[2]See Florence L. Huey, "How Nurses Would Change U.S. Health Care," *American Journal of Nursing,* November 1988, pp. 1482-93.

[3]Sonia Umanzor, "Nightmare in El Salvador," *Journal of Christian Nursing,* Spring 1986, pp. 10-12.

[4]See Ronald J. Sider, *Rich Christians in an Age of Hunger* (Downers Grove, Ill.: InterVarsity Press, 1977), pp. 31-56, for an extensive treatment of this problem.

[5]Brian Bird, "Christians Who Grow Coca," *Christianity Today,* September 8, 1989, pp. 40-43.

[6]Alan Bauer, "Education: a Key in Halting Domestic Violence," *The Boyertown Area Times,* February 1, 1990, p. 1.

[7]Barbara Simsen, "In Perspective," *Christian Nurse International,* 5(4), 1989, p. 3.

[8]Irene Schomus, "The Consequences of Crushing Poverty: A Nurse Fights Back," *Journal of Christian Nursing,* Summer 1984, p. 11.

[9]Janet Fuller, "Lethal Dose: Should a Nurse Resist Doctor's Orders?" *Journal of Christian Nursing,* Fall 1986, pp. 4-8.

[10]Arthur Simon, *Christian Faith and Public Policy: No Grounds for Divorce* (Grand Rapids, Mich.: W. B. Eerdmans, 1987), p. 106.

[11]For more information about Parish Nursing see *The Journal of Christian Nursing,* Winter 1989, pp. 26-33; Granger Westberg with Jill Westberg McNamara, *The Parish Nurse: How to Start a Parish Nurse Program in Your Church* (Park Ridge, Ill.: Parish Nurse Resource Center, 1987); or write to The Parish Nurse Resource Center, Parkside Center, 1875 Dempster St., Park Ridge, IL 60068.

[12]Richard John Neuhaus, *Christian Faith and Public Policy: Thinking and Acting*

in the Courage of Uncertainty (Minneapolis: Augsburg, 1977), p. 52.
[13]Philip D. Yancey, "The Embattled Career of Dr. Koop," *Christianity Today*, October 20, 1989, p. 21.
[14]Ann Connor, "More Than a Home: One Nurse's Vision of a Healing Community," *Journal of Christian Nursing*, Fall 1988, pp. 17-18.

Chapter Ten: Christian Nursing in a Secular Profession
[1]Scholars use the term *civil religion* to refer to "a way of thinking which makes sacred a political arrangement or governmental system and provides a religious image of a political society for many, if not most of its members. . . .

"In short it is the social glue which binds a given society together by means of well-established ceremonies—rituals, symbols, values—and allegiances which function in the life of the community in such a way as to provide it with an overarching sense of spiritual unity. Therefore, it is not a particular or specific religion or expression thereof, but is of such a nature that those who hold specific beliefs can read into it whatever meaning they choose. . . .

"Over the years the American civic faith has grown conceptually from evangelical Protestantism-in-general to Christianity-in-general, to the Judeo-Christian tradition, to theism-in-general." From R. D. Linder, "Civil Religion," in Daniel G. Reid, Robert D. Linder, Bruce L. Shelley, and Harry S. Stout, eds., *Dictionary of Christianity in America* (Downers Grove, Ill.: InterVarsity Press, 1990), pp. 281-82.
[2]Elsie L. and Bertram Bandman, "Ethical Aspects of Nursing," Chapter 12 in Janet-Beth Flynn and Phyllis Heffron, *Nursing: From Concept to Practice* (Norwalk: Appleton & Lange, 1988).
[3]Joyce G. Baldwin, *Daniel: An Introduction and Commentary* (Downers Grove, Ill.: InterVarsity Press, 1978), p. 83.
[4]John E. Goldingay, *Daniel*, vol. 30 in *Word Biblical Commentary* (Dallas: Word Book Publishers, 1989), pp. 329-34.
[5]Baldwin, *Daniel*, p. 12.